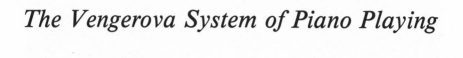

The Vengerova System of Piano Playing

Vengerova in her studio on her seventy-fifth birthday.

The Vengerova System of Piano Playing

Robert D. Schick

The Pennsylvania State University Press
University Park and London

Library of Congress Cataloging in Publication Data
Schick, Robert D.
The Vengerova system of piano playing.
Includes bibliography and index.
1. Piano — Methods.   2. Vengerova, Isabelle.
II. Title.
MT222.S34   786.3'041   82-80454
ISBN 0-271-00313-8   AACR2

CONTENTS

PHOTOGRAPHS

Preface

By the time I began studying with Isabelle Vengerova (vehn-geh'-roh-vah) in New York City in 1944, her name had acquired an almost legendary quality among pianists. Some of the talk centered about her great number of talented pupils who were winning contests and playing important engagements. Often people discussed her demanding personality, her biting wit, and her frequent outbursts of temper. Conversation focussed on her system of technique and how it helped her pupils achieve the coveted goal of an entrée into the world of concert pianism.

At that time Olga Samaroff was her chief rival among the doyennes of piano teaching. Certainly theirs were the names I heard mentioned most often. In the true fashion of teenagers my friends and I debated the merits of who was better, though probably with more enthusiasm than wisdom, since none of us had studied with both, and our knowledge of the other teacher was usually based on questionable hearsay.

The years have passed since then, and Vengerova and Samaroff are both deceased. New stars in the world of piano teaching have appeared and, in some cases, have already faded away after their burst of glory.

Nevertheless, I have written this book now because Vengerova had something that endured, an extraordinary and highly developed system of technique and tone production which she apparently evolved on her own. This method is still valid even though she is no longer here, and is used by many of her pupils (including myself) in their playing and teaching. A knowledge of it could still be of tremendous value to pianists today. Until now none of the writings about her has given to this aspect of her teaching the detailed attention it needs and deserves. I hope this book will serve that function.

There is, however, an additional goal to this study. It has been organized so that one could almost learn to play the piano from it even if one's method of tone production differs radically from Vengerova's. The sections on pedaling, fingering, legato and staccato touches, singing tone, as well as those on the practicing of etudes, scales, arpeggios, double notes, octaves (legato and staccato), and leaps should be helpful to all students from the intermediate level on, and equally useful to their teachers.

It would be well to mention the names of some of her pupils who achieved renown. These include Gary Graffman, Lilian Kallir, Jacob Lateiner, Zadel Skolovsky, Sylvia Zaremba, Gilbert Kalish, Anthony di Bonaventura, Sidney Foster, and Abba Bogin. Others, while still performing as pianists from time to time, are better known today for their careers as composers or conductors. This list includes Samuel Barber, Leonard Bernstein, Lukas Foss, and Thomas Scherman. Some additional figures of importance are Ralph Berkowitz, Annette Elkanova, Eileen Flissler, Jean Graham, Judith Jaimes, Jose Kahan, Sol Kaplan, Gilbert Kalish, Sylvan Levin, Harry Lee Neal, Patricia Parr, Teresa Qusada, Joseph Rezits, Irene Rosenberg, Harriet Serr, Harriet Shirvan, Florence Frantz Vennett Snyder, and Ronald Turini. (The names of those who only coached with her are not listed.)

This book is based on the detailed notes I took during the period of almost ten years when I was Vengerova's pupil. I am thankful, however, for the invaluable assistance given to me by many people. Places of honor must be reserved for three individuals: Vengerova's assistant, Florence Frantz Vennett Snyder; Lilian Kallir; and Vengerova's nephew, the noted musicologist and lexicographer, Nicolas Slonimsky. Mrs. Snyder and Miss Kallir gave me useful information about Vengerova's teaching and, what is even more important, astute advice at a crucial stage of the writing which helped determine the shape of the book. Mr. Slonimsky provided me with details of his aunt's personal life and professional background which I could not have otherwise obtained. These included translations from the Russian and authorizations to reproduce both Jacob Millstein's brief biography of Vengerova and the unpublished article about her early years as a teacher by the late musicologist, Vitaly Neumann.

Let me express my appreciation to Vengerova's other assistants who helped me: Olga Stroumillo, Barbara Elliott Bailey, Helen Schafranek; and to Jacob Lateiner for answering my questions about Vengerova's approach to teaching octaves and trills.

My thanks are given also to Chris W. Kentera and John M. Pickering of the Pennsylvania State University Press; to John de Lancie, Director of the Curtis Institute of Music, for his encouragement and support; to Thomas Reed who took the photographs of my hands illustrating various positions at the keyboard; to Rita H. Mead for her work as an editor; to Elizabeth Walker, music librarian of the Curtis Institute of Music; to John Gaunt and Charles Sprenkle for their helpful readings of the nearly-completed manuscript; to my wife, Ruth, for her assistance in many ways; and to William Holcombe, who prepared the musical examples.

Robert D. Schick
West Chester, Pennsylvania
January 1982

Chapter I

Vengerova: the Person and the Teacher

A brief biography of Vengerova, written by Jacob Millstein, appeared in Russia in the "Annual Bulletin of Memorable Musical Events for 1977" published by *Musyka*.[1] I now present it with a few additions of my own in brackets, and some corrections of dates:

ON MARCH 1, 1977, ONE HUNDRED YEARS SINCE THE BIRTH OF ISABELLE AFANASIEVNA VENGEROVA (1877-1956)

I. A. Vengerova was born in Minsk, in a highly cultured family. She attracted attention as a child by her unusual musical gift. After graduation from high school in Minsk, Vengerova went to Vienna, where she entered the Vienna Conservatory. She completed her studies there as pianist in the class of Joseph Dachs; later she took a special course for two years with Leschetizky in Vienna and subsequently with Anna Essipova in St. Petersburg. In 1904 she passed the examination at the St. Petersburg Conservatory for the degree of "free artist." Her pedagogical activities began in Kiev in the late 1890s after her return from Vienna. And it was in Kiev where she began her concert career, first in chamber music, then as a soloist. From 1900 on she lived in St. Petersburg, and continued to appear in symphonic, chamber music and solo concerts. The critics noted in her playing a substantive quality, fine taste and a broad artistic culture. Her innate musicianship was never in question, and soon she gained recognition among the most fastidious listeners. [With Kochanski and Joseph Press she took part in a Brahms cycle in St. Petersburg, playing for the first time in Russia most of the chamber works of that composer.] In 1906 she was appointed assistant [to Mme. Essipova] in the piano department of the St. Petersburg Conservatory, and in 1910 was appointed Professor. From 1923 on she lived in the United States, mostly in New York and in Philadelphia, where she obtained the reputation of a brilliant pedagogue. During many years she taught [beginning 1924], along with Josef Hofmann and others, at the Curtis Institute of Philadelphia. [That institution granted her an honorary doctorate in 1950. She was also on the faculty of the Mannes College of Music in New York.] She was an enthusiastic teacher, possessing a truly maternal love for her students.

[1]Nicolas Slonimsky, who sent me this biography and made its translation, said that Millstein was a well known Russian pianist who studied with Igumnov in Moscow and wrote an excellent biography of Liszt.

She taught intelligently, interestingly, originally and masterfully. She had definite methodical principles aimed at the cultivation of the individual gifts of her students and at the development among them of spontaneous musical thinking. Among her pupils were Samuel Barber, Leonard Bernstein, Lukas Foss and other important American Musicians. Vengerova died in New York [of cancer on February 7, 1956], shortly before reaching her seventy-ninth birthday.[2]

Vengerova continued to perform as well as teach after she arrived in the United States. When she played the Schumann Concerto with the Detroit Symphony in that city on February 8, 1925, the reviewer for *Musical America,* Mabel McDonough Furney, reported that "she showed remarkable technical facility and a tone characterized by an ingratiating sweetness."[3] It is difficult, however, to trace the record of her performing career in this country, aside from the various programs she gave at Curtis, because her scrapbook has disappeared. Although her last solo recital probably took place in New York City in 1944 or 1945, the latest program I have located is the chamber music concert she gave with Joseph Fuchs, violinist, and Felix Salmond, 'cellist, on May 6, 1944 at the New York Public Library on Forty-second Street in New York City. It was part of the "Victory Concert" series "For Men in the Service and Their Companions." They played the Mendelssohn Trio in D Minor and the Brahms Trio in C Major. Less than a month earlier, on April 18, 1944, she had played the same Mendelssohn trio and the Tschaikowsky Trio in A Minor at Curtis Hall in Philadelphia with Efrem Zimbalist, violinist, and Gregor Piatigorsky, 'cellist.

Vengerova came from a distinguished family. Her father Hanan was a banker and community worker in Minsk. Her mother Pauline attracted much attention with her *Memoirs of a Grandmother: Pictures of the Cultural History of Russian Jews in the Nineteenth Century,* published between 1908 and 1910. Vengerova's sister Zinaida was a well-known literary critic and writer on Russian culture, and a brother Semyon was a literary and intellectural historian, as well as a bibliogra-

---

[2]The dates of Vengerova's appointment at the St. Petersburg Conservatory have been changed to those given in the sixth edition of *Baker's Biographical Dictionary of Musicians* which was compiled by Slonimsky himself. The reference to her honorary doctorate also comes from there as well as the date when she started at Curtis. Her age at death also had to be corrected.

The information about the Brahms cycle in which she took part comes from material about her on file in the library of the Curtis Institute of Music. The significant fact that she was Mme. Essipova's assistant is mentioned there in several biographies prepared for publication.

[3]"Detroit Symphony Gains New Success," *Musical America* 41 (February 8, 1925):9.

pher and editor of reference books. [4]

In reply to my question about whether Vengerova had ever been married, Nicolas Slonimsky stated:

> No, my aunt was never married, although she had several old-world liaisons, some of them stormy. Her first was her second cousin Leo Van Jung of Vienna; that was over with the outbreak of World War I, when my aunt was in Russia, and Van Jung stayed in Vienna. Her last was the violinist Michael Press, and that went on in New York from 1923 to about 1932. Many distinguished musicians and literary men courted her during the period between 1897 and 1914, but she invariably selected the worst ones who never took care of her. She had many platonic admirers in Vienna, among them the author of *Bambi*, the children's classic; when she was very young she was introduced to Brahms who kissed her on the brow.

The Vengerova of later years was a complex and fascinating being, though undoubtedly one who was changed in many ways from what she was in the days of her colorful past. There were many sides to her personality, not all of which would be readily evident to any one individual.

When I first met her she was a heavy-set woman in her middle sixties whose face still revealed how pretty she must have been when young. In public she was austere and severe in manner, as she often was with students, though there were many moments when she relaxed. At her most appealing she had a twinkle in her eye, a warm smile, and a sense of humor, as well as affection and concern for her pupils. But there is no denying that it was often a difficult experience emotionally for many to work with her, for Vengerova also had her weaknesses.

Certainly her chief faults were the sharp and acid tongue and the ferocious temper she displayed at times towards many of her students. A few examples of her biting remarks are included in the obituary by Jay S. Harrison, reprinted in Appendix A. Others can be found in the writings of her pupils Joseph Rezits and Harry Lee Neal. An analysis of this side of her personality, however, is no simple matter, and no two interpretations will completely agree.

Thomas Scherman, the conductor, was quoted as follows in Mr. Harrison's obituary:

> She was a tremendous disciplinarian, so much so that a great many potential students couldn't take the rules she insisted on. . .She was a sensitive psychologist and treated each student as a distinct case. I think she could have stopped teaching at any time and become a psychologist and made a fortune.

[4] *Encyclopaedia Judaica,* s.v. "Wengeroff, Pauline," by Yehuda Slutzky, and "Wengeroff (Vengerov), Semyon Afanasyevich," by Maurice Friedberg.

For one thing, she took each pupil individually—and though she had a distinct teaching method it could be applied to each student differently. She also acted as an artistic conscience for every pupil until each could develop a conscience of his own.

It would never have occurred to me, however, to call her a sensitive psychologist, although there is undoubtedly a strange truth to the statement. To me a sensitive psychologist has concern for the feelings of others, and this is where Vengerova was often at her worst. Although the discipline she required often accomplished remarkable things, a kinder approach would have worked better for many.

It must be emphasized, though, that she varied her approach to pupils on a personal level. All were not treated with cruelty or excessive harshness.

She was a very demanding teacher even when young, according to what her nephew Nicolas Slonimsky told me, though he still recalled with great affection his lessons with her.[5] She was also a product of an old-fashioned authoritarian European tradition. For instance, she expected from most of her pupils an absolute and unquestioning obedience and adherence to her ideas, both technical and musical, which made it difficult from them to grow on their own.

Although in many ways a superb musician, she also had some musical limitations. For instance, her conceptions of Bach and Mozart revealed that her roots were in the last century, and that she was largely unfamiliar with the work of those scholars who were unearthing the performance practices of the eighteenth century. Nevertheless, I must add that I remember much that was fine in her Mozart, such as the strength and authority with which she began the C Minor Sonata, and the delicacy of her shadings in so many places.

It must be noted, too, that she had adopted the twentieth-century practice of insisting that all of the markings in the music be followed meticulously. This is a generally admirable philosophy when done with an understanding of their meanings. Unfortunately, it became awkward to carry out at times, for Vengerova retained an old-fashioned affection for edited versions of music rather than Urtexts, and these two characteristics of her teaching did not combine well.

Why did so many of her students remain despite these problems, and why did new ones keep flocking to her door? The exact reason undoubtedly varied from person to person, but in most cases it probably was because they knew of nobody else who had such ability to mold a raw talent into a professional performer.

[5]A description of them is found in his article " 'Musique': Reminiscences of a vanished world," *The Piano Teacher* 6 (September-October 1963): 2-4.

How did she accomplish this? What were the other strengths that made her such a vital force in the world of piano teaching? Among them was a sharp awareness of her goals, both musical and technical, and a knowledge of ways to achieve them. This applies both to the immediate aim of learning particular works well and to the long range one of developing pupils who had a fine command of their instrument and its literature, and who might, in many cases, be ready for a career on the concert stage.

She knew well what was needed to build a pupil's technique and musicianship, including what works to assign from her enormous repertoire. Although many of her pupils were advanced, she was not adverse to teaching talented beginners. However, by the end of her life her assistants probably did most of the work with the youngsters.

Her ear was extraordinarily keen. She could spot a pedal that was held a fraction too long, or a chord that was out of balance, or a slight but unwanted accent in a melody, and then work relentlessly on the passage until it was pedaled, balanced, and phrased with subtlety and character.

Though often ailing in her last years, she still taught with an intensity that could wear out a pupil by the end of the hour. She could work at great length on details, and yet at the proper moment would turn her attention towards pulling the work together so as to achieve a magical flow of line and tempo.

She was able to play beautifully until the very end. During the last decade of her life this was achieved without any practice aside from what was obtained by demonstrating at a lesson. (Her devoted maid, Anna, confirmed what Vengerova had told me in this regard.) Of course, some passages now evaded her, but most, including some of great difficulty, were admirable.

Indeed I firmly believe that in her later years Vengerova's teaching profited in many ways because she no longer practiced. She was still proud of her ability as a pianist, and so was forced to discover ways to maintain this only by demonstrating at lessons. These insights would then be passed on to her pupils. If a phrase did not go particularly well when she first played it, she would try to make some adjustment of arm weight or wrist position, etc., so that it would sound better on the repetition. She made her students use the same approach. While she certainly emphasized that lots of practice was necessary, she often had us make a correction instantly at a lesson when knowledge of the proper procedure alone could bring about the improvement.

Since Vengerova always taught seated at a second piano whose keyboard was adjacent to and continuous with the one where the student sat, there could be a constant interplay without interruption between her demonstration and the student's imitation. However, she did not depend only on rote teaching, but also made her points with great skill verbally.

Her lessons usually began with technical material such as scales and arpeggios. This would usually be omitted, however, if the student was advanced or was studying with an assistant. Then an etude would be performed. This would be played through without interruption, although Vengerova might make a comment, perhaps about tempo or dynamics, or else play along briefly in a way suggesting a different sonority or touch, and the student was supposed to make the correction without breaking the rhythm. I suspect, too, that sometimes she played along merely to give herself a bit of practice. What she would do next depended upon the changes that were needed.

She would then listen to the pieces, usually hearing each one in its entirety before suggesting any changes. If the work was long she might make some notes on a pad during the initial performance.

It was not necessary to memorize a new composition for the first lesson, nor to play a fast work up to tempo. She demanded, however, a reasonable degree of rhythmic continuity and expected a sizeable portion of the work, usually a movement, to be prepared. (At one time, though, in Russia, she apparently expected all pieces to be memorized for the first lesson. See Appendix C., p. 108.)

One of the fascinating aspects of Vengerova's teaching is the way musical and technical principles were so completely interwoven with one another. (By musical principles I mean such things as the ways to achieve good phrasing and balance, to set and modify tempi (including rubato), to adjust interpretations according to the needs of different composers and styles, and to project the structure and character of a piece by dynamics.) She always seemed ready to reinforce a musical point with a suggestion on how to achieve the effect technically. Yet she was also concerned that the technique be at the service of the music. Those who said that technique was her chief interest did not realize how aware she was that technique alone will sound sterile, dry, and even lacking in brilliance if it is not applied to a musical goal which will give it the needed color, sheen, and sparkle. Music and technique must work together towards a joint end.

It is partly because of this that Vengerova's musical principles will usually appear in relation to points being made about technique or another of her specialties, pedaling. There is no separate section per se on her musical ideas. But there are other reasons for this besides the interrelationship of her musical and technical points.

One of them is the nature of the notes I took throughout my study with Vengerova, except for the first year and a half. After a lesson I would write down the points that had been made, either in a notebook or in my music. But while my records of her remarkable technical system are clear-cut and easy to convert into generalizations, those of her musical ideas apply more to particular passages and are more difficult to state as basic principles.

It is possible that I had absorbed many of the concepts and only needed to record some specific applications. Then, too, Vengerova never created a musical system as unique and highly organized as her technical one, except in those areas where her musical and technical ideas were closely interwoven. This makes it harder for me to separate her musical ideas from those I acquired throughout the years by contact with other teachers and performers.

Another problem is that many of Vengerova's musical points dealt with the details needed to achieve a more elegant phrasing, balance, tone, or tempo. Such instructions often cannot be reduced to words alone, or to meaningful generalizations when one gets beyond basic and obvious points. They need the world of sound to survive.

Vengerova's playing also had a fine legato, warmth of singing tone, and graciousness and charm (where appropriate) which was a major influence on her pupils. One would need recordings of her lessons—unfortunately I know of none—to get a more complete view of these sides of her teaching.

Her remarkable technical system, however, survives very well by itself. It is an approach that can be learned and taught by others. Indeed, from the 1930s on, Vengerova was aided in handling her large class of pupils by a group of assistants, at least three of whom, Florence Frantz Vennett Snyder, Harriet Serr, and in particular Zadel Skolovsky, also achieved some renown as performers. Her other assistants were Olga Stroumillo, Barbara Elliott Bailey, and the late Mildred Jones. A close friend, Helen Schafranek, also functioned in that capacity at times. Miss Schafranek told me that she was actually given the title of assistant, but this occurred so close to Vengerova's death that it had little significance. There may have been others, too, in the earlier days, particularly in Russia, whose names are unknown to me.

The assistants taught more than just technique, for they worked on the same pieces as did Vengerova. While inevitably some problems and occasional confusion would arise because a pupil had two teachers, these were kept to a minimum because all of the instruction took place within the framework of the same system.

The assistants, however, usually did not assign the literature. That role was reserved for Vengerova. Although advanced pupils were permitted to select their own pieces, she often supplemented their choices with her own suggestions.

There were many advantages to being a Vengerova assistant, most notably that of being sent a constant stream of talented pupils. However, one had to teach the way Vengerova did, and those who wanted to develop their own style of teaching might have found this a drawback.

I have spoken to three assistants about this. Two of them had no serious problems. Initially Mrs. Snyder was concerned about what Vengerova would want her to say, but she soon discovered that if she just told the student what she thought the work needed, Madame would be pleased. Barbara Elliott Bailey found it natural to teach that way because Vengerova's approach had proven effective for solving musical and pianistic problems in her own playing.

It was surprising to me to learn that Olga Stroumillo, who was also Vengerova's closest friend during the period in which I knew them, and whom many perceived as the symbol of orthodox adherence to Vengerova's principles, found that being an assistant was confining. However, having agreed to take on that role she continued to teach as was expected of her while Vengerova was alive. Since Vengerova's death she has modified her approach to piano instruction and no longer follows Vengerova's system of practicing with accents.

There undoubtedly must be a strong tendency for an assistant to become more orthodox than the teacher.[6] For example, Vengerova could break the rules when she saw good reason to do so, for she was the person who made them up. Her assistants could not be so flexible, for fear that Vengerova would not have liked what was being done and would criticize the poor student for deviating from her technique.

I hope, though, that my description of her teaching and technical system does not make it appear more rigid than it was. It is important to realize that while her students had to stay within the confines of her technical approach, within these limits Vengerova was extraordinarily creative, imaginative, and flexible, and she encouraged her students to be the same. Otherwise, they could never have achieved such success.

When I first began to study with Vengerova in the fall of 1944 at the

[6]For a brief discussion of this topic see Egon Petri's "Problems of Piano Playing and Teaching" in Robert E. Simon, ed., *Be Your Own Music Critic* (Garden City, NY: Doubleday, Doran and Co., Inc., 1941), pp. 139-40.

8

age of fifteen, I worked exclusively with her except for two or three lessons with an assistant. This continued for a year. Later I usually studied with an assistant between my lessons with Madame. During the last two years of her life I again worked only with her. (At all times my lessons with Vengerova were arranged privately and not through a school.)

The total duration of my training with her was about eleven and one-half years, from the fall of 1944 until January 1956, a month before her death. During this time there were two periods when I was unable to work with her: from February 1946 to September 1947, largely because of my formal education, and for about eight months in 1953-54 immediately after my being drafted into the Army.

I worked at different times with four assistants, Mildred Jones, Florence Frantz Vennett Snyder, Olga Stroumillo, and Zadel Skolovsky, all of whom were fine teachers.[7] Nevertheless, this book is based mainly on the ideas that were given to me directly by Vengerova. My notes on my lessons were helpful here since they usually distinguished her remarks from those of an assistant. When a point emanates from an assistant this has been indicated in the text. The musical examples are all from pieces I studied with Vengerova with but one clearly marked exception.

According to Mrs. Snyder and Dr. Bailey, Vengerova denied having a formal method, though most pianists would probably think she did. If we mean by method an "orderly, logical, effective plan or procedure,"[8] her approach to teaching must qualify as one.

Although much of it is original and different, this is not true of all. Many of her ideas are shared by good pianists and teachers everywhere, for it would be impossible to create a completely new approach to the piano which would work.

As a student I often wondered about the origins of her method, in particular those of her way of practicing with accents, which will be described shortly. But I never had the courage to ask Madame about it for fear she might interpret the question as being unnecessarily personal and perhaps impertinent. I have since asked many of her pupils and associates about it, without finding a definitive answer.

---

[7]This was an unusually large number of assistants for one pupil, since most of her students probably studied only with one. It was brought about by a variety of circumstances of little significance today—which assistant's schedule had more room, where I was living at the time, and so on.

[8]*Webster's Third New International Dictionary of the English Language Unabridged,* s.v. "Method."

Olga Stroumillo, her close friend and assistant, said that Vengerova once stated that she had been teaching that way for so long she could not remember herself. Mme. Stroumillo then suggested that I ask Vengerova's nephew, Nicolas Slonimsky. When I did so he replied that he thought it came from Leschetizky.

The writings about Leschetizky by his students suggest, however, that he taught different individuals in different ways, and that he let his pupils utilize a greater variety of piano techniques than did Vengerova. Nothing suggests that he required a system of practicing like hers.[9]

Barbara Elliott Bailey thought that the method might have come from Anna Essipova, the second of Leschetizky's wives, his assistant for a while, and a famous pianist in her own right. (Vengerova had studied with her in St. Petersburg after leaving Leschetizky, and later became her assistant.)[10] But Artur Schnabel, who began studying with

---

[9]The best-known book about Leschetizky's teaching is *The Groundwork of the Leschetizky Method, Issued with His Approval by His Assistant Malwine Brée* (New York: G. Schirmer, 1902). For a general discussion of Leschetizky's approach to playing and technique see Chapter 13 in Reginald Gerig, *Famous Pianists and Their Technique* (Washington: Robert B. Luce, Inc., 1974). Gerig gives other sources of information about Leschetizky.

Artur Schnabel, a Leschetizky pupil, had lessons with about a half-dozen of his assistants. Schnabel said, "They differed in pianistic functions as much as one can differ, and were also not at all unanimous in their approach to music. Each, of course, called his conception the true Leschetizky method. Several published books on it. If a student were to read all these books he would get a considerable demonstration of confusion." *My Life and Music* (New York: St. Martin's Press, 1963), p. 26. Reproduced by permission.

This contrasts sharply with the way Vengerova's assistants had to use her technical method exclusively.

[10]Dr. Bailey was struck by the resemblance between some descriptions of Essipova's playing when she appeared in the United States in 1876-77 and the character of Vengerova's own performances. Here are two excerpts from one review:

> Her shapely arms, bare to the shoulder, show a remarkable development of the forearm and wrist, and this it is which enables her to play, as she does, entirely from the elbow and wrist, avoiding the awkward appearance of moving the shoulders or the body... .

> Add to the merits already enumerated, a most amazing brilliancy and ease of execution, perfect accuracy and a touch altogether phenomenal, and you will have a faint idea of some of the least of those qualities which mark the playing of this great artiste. Without dwelling too long upon those qualities which are, to the real worth of her playing, only as the stepping stones to the sanctuary, mention must be made of her touch, *i.e.*, of the quality of the tone which she produces from the instrument; since Gottschalk sang his way into our heart with syren fingers we have heard nothing to equal it. Mme. Essipoff is able to produce from the piano, to suit the

Leschetizky in 1891 at the age of nine, though he worked mainly with Essipova during the first year, reported that "She used to put a coin on my hand, a silver coin almost as big as a silver dollar (a gulden) and if I played one Czerny study without dropping it, she gave it to me as a present."[11] As will be seen later, this bears no resemblance to Vengerova's approach to practicing an etude.

There is probably no simple explanation to the origins of her system of technique. Vengerova may have absorbed ideas from many different sources throughout the years, while adding some concepts of her own.[12] (She herself claimed this, according to Mrs. Snyder.) Gradually these principles, both those that were borrowed and those that were original with her, may have coalesced into the distinctive approach to playing which is described in this volume.

varying moods of a composer, a great variety of tone, as if she had changed her instrument repeatedly. Her runs and arpeggios are as clear and sparkling as the musical glasses; her chords are like a single note; while her legato must be heard to be appreciated.

Review of Essipova's debut in Steinway Hall in New York City on November 14, 1876, signed by A.A.C. *Dwight's Journal of Music* 36 (November 25, 1876): 343.

[11]Schnabel, *My Life and Music,* p. 11. Reproduced by permission.

[12]Vengerova apparently had read some writers who analyzed the merits of different piano techniques using the terminology of physics, in particular the laws of levers. She once justified one aspect of her technique—her insistence on keeping the elbow quiet when playing an accent—using expressions like "a shorter distance from the fulcrum."

Chapter II

A Summary of Her Technique

The proper production of a sound is the basis of her technique, and provides the foundation for the development of speed, flexibility, and power. All of the following points relate at least in part to her method of tone production.

(1) Non-percussive touch. The fingers are to be close to the keys and in contact with them before playing. (This rule is disregarded only when playing a hand staccato.)

(2) Flexible wrist. The flexibility and power of the wrist must be developed.

(3) Accents. It is important to be able to play an accent in any context desired. To produce an accent the wrist is raised and the fingertip prepared on the key. The hand is held firmly from the fingertips through the knuckles to the wrist, though without unnecessary tension before making the sound. At the moment of tone production the wrist is pushed sharply downward with its energy going into the fingertip and then into the key. (The tone should not be harsh, however.) One relaxes immediately afterward.

(4) Quiet upper arm. At no time is the upper arm used directly in the production of an accent. (Her technique differs sharply in this regard from that of some other schools of piano playing.) When playing an accent the power comes from the application to the key of pressure from the finger and wrist. The elbow stays in a relatively fixed position, and the upper arm remains quiet.

(5) Relaxation. All muscles must be relaxed while playing except for those directly involved in tone production. These, too, should be relaxed immediately afterward.

(6) Weight. The correct application of weight into the key is essential. One directs a greater amount of weight into the keyboard for loud sounds, and a lesser amount for soft ones.

(7) Applications to music. The hand must follow the fingers in whatever pattern they play. (Indeed the proper hand motion can help the fingers find their notes.) At the same time the weight is transferred from one key to the next. When combined with a "close to the keys," non-percussive touch, these principles help to produce a good legato.

Vengerova in Vienna in 1898. The inscription, "To my teacher of life from his unsuccessful pupil," was apparently written to her second cousin, the Viennese pianist, Leo van Jung.

13

To my darling young friend and talented assistant with love and wishes for success.

Isabelle Vengerova

June, 1949

New York

Blanche de Lorière

This picture, for many years the best-known one of Vengerova, appeared in *Musical Courier* on November 12, 1932. The dedication here is to Barbara Elliott Bailey.

An undated photograph of Vengerova from the files of the Curtis Institute of Music.

Vengerova and the ten-year old Gary Graffman. This photograph appeared in *Life* on December 12, 1938 in an article about music instruction in the United States. (Reproduced by permission of the photographer and copyright holder, Fritz Henle.)

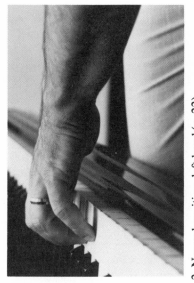

2. Normal position, left hand (p. 22).

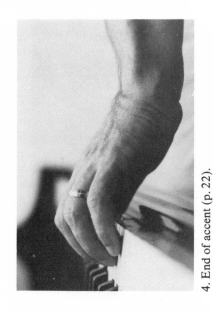

4. End of accent (p. 22).

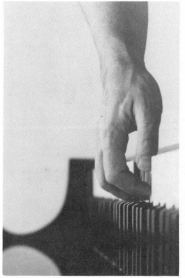

1. Normal position, right hand (p. 22).

3. Preparation of accent (p.22).

17

6. Position for singing tone (p. 46).

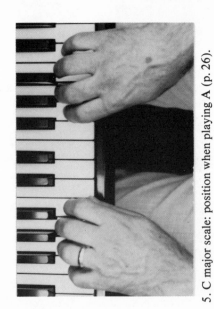

5. C major scale: position when playing A (p. 26).

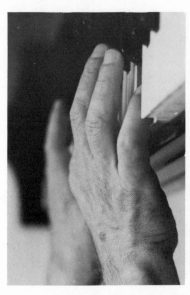

8. Correct way to play melody with chords (p. 47).

7. Incorrect way to play melody with chords (p. 47).

10. Playing C ascending or G descending.

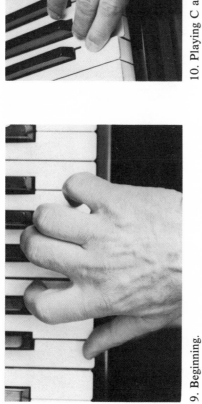

9. Beginning.

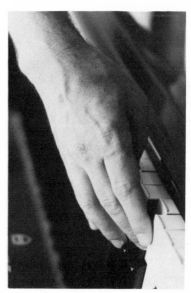

11. Same position as 10., a second view

12. Same position as 10., a third view.

Positions for C major arpeggio (p. 53).

19

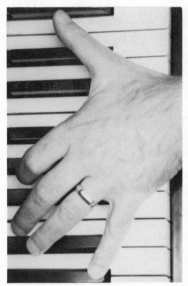

13. Position for legato thirds (p. 60).

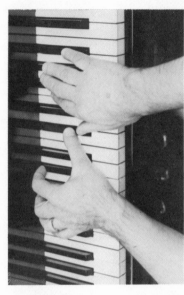

14. Position for leaps (p. 63).

15. Curvature of thumb first joint (p. 72).

16. Position for Chopin Scherzo (p. 83).

Chapter III

The Basics of the System

INTRODUCTION

A perusal of the table of contents will indicate that the organization of this book gives Vengerova's approach to various aspects of piano playing—scales, arpeggios, double notes, staccato, etc. Except for the discussion of pedaling, which can stand by itself, an understanding of this chapter and the next helps one comprehend what comes later. Once it has been acquired, however, those topics can be read out of sequence and still be meaningful.

Vengerova probably varied the order in which she introduced this material to her students, for she would adjust her teaching to their needs at the moment and to their levels of advancement, as all good teachers do. A few words are appropriate, though, insofar as one can generalize, about how she would teach new students.[13]

(1) She would work to help them relax physically by her choice of exercises and selection of literature. (One of the first pieces she assigned me, Chopin's Etude in A^b, Op. 25, No. 1 ("Aeolian Harp"), was an excellent choice for that purpose.) (2) Improving legato was one of her important goals, too. (3) In my case she began teaching her system of accents, which is so basic to her tone production, at the very first lesson, though Mrs. Snyder says this was not always so with other students. (4) Compositions to develop a singing tone would also be given early in the course of study.

Many practice procedures learned by students before coming to Vengerova could still be retained. One could still play a piece, or a passage from it, in a musical way below tempo. All practicing did not have to be with her accents, even though that is a central feature of her system, as will be seen shortly.

---

[13]Most of Vengerova's instructions to her assistants on teaching were probably given verbally. In the early 1930s, however, she wrote Mrs. Snyder the following about a student just beginning at Curtis: "give her a lesson...[on] hand position, relaxation, approach to the keys. Her technic is superficial and the touch without variety. Give: 1) drop of whole hand on three and four fingers [Exercise 3e, p. 33]; 2) stops on thumb/close fingers in down movement of the right, up movement of the left [part of Exercise 3n, p. 35]; 3) every note with [a] big swing [Exercise 3f, p. 33]; 4) scales with accents and so on."

A. Posture and Hand Position

When one plays a basic five finger position in both hands on the white keys, the body should be placed far enough away from the keyboard so that the elbows can pass easily in front when the left hand moves toward the treble register or the right hand toward the bass. The height of the chair should be adjusted so that the bottom of the thumb and wrist can rest comfortably in the same plane as the top of the depressed key.

The third finger (the longest) is nearest the black keys, the second and fourth fingers a little behind, the fifth finger about midway between the edge of the white keys and the black keys, and the thumb placed with just its nail on the key. The knuckles are arched, and the hand is held level so that it does not tilt toward either the thumb or fifth finger. (See photos 1 and 2, p. 17.)

In order to get the correct hand position, Vengerova told me to reverse the hand so that the back is down and the palm up, as if holding a ball, and then to place the hand on the keyboard, maintaining the same shape, with the fingers over adjacent white keys. One can use the reflection in the board behind the keys to check on hand position.

B. Accents on Every Note ("Ones")

The student is first introduced to the Vengerova system of technique and tone production by learning how to play an accent on every note of a basic five finger position. This is called "playing in 'ones' " in Vengerova terminology. The five finger pattern would then be expanded, perhaps at the first lesson, to a scale of one octave. However, my description will be restricted initially to the five finger position to avoid the problems presented by the passing of the thumb.

(1) Use of wrist. To play an accent the wrist is raised as high as possible beforehand but without losing the curvature of the fingers. (See photo 3, p. 17.) The fingertip then presses firmly into the key, and the wrist drives down sharply and quickly at the same time in a strictly vertical plane. At the end of the accent the wrist will be considerably lower than when it began, but it should not go much lower, if at all, than the basic position of the hand described above, in which the bottom of the thumb rests comfortably in the same plane as the top of the depressed key. (See photo 4, p. 17.) Certainly the motion should stop long before the hand hits the board in front of the keys, for that could be uncomfortable.

The wrist must be used in a controlled way so that an accent can be played without strain or effort beyond the minimum work required of well-trained muscles to produce the sound.

Since the wrist must move a longer distance than the fingertip, which can only move as far as the key descends, and since both begin their motions simultaneously, the wrist motion continues past the moment when the sound is produced. This resembles the follow-through motion of a baseball batter who continues his movement after hitting the ball. In order to play another accent the wrist is then raised in preparation as before. Details about this will be given later on.

(One could argue that the sounds that emerge from a series of tones like those described above should not really be called accents, since an accent is a note that stands out from its neighbors, and none of these do. This looseness of terminology is harmless, however, since one is learning a technique that will be used to produce an accent in the proper context.)

(2) Fingertip preparation on key. The fingertip must be in contact with the key at all times. The basic Vengerova touch is a prepared, non-percussive one.

(3) Weight and relaxation. One must feel the arm weight going into the fingertip and the key when playing an accent. Mme. Vengerova once told me to imagine that a ton was suddenly placed on my wrist forcing it down, with the pressure going into the fingertip and then into the key. One relaxes immediately afterward—this cannot be overemphasized —with the fingertip maintaining just the small amount of pressure that is needed to hold the key down.

(4) Legato. One must carefully connect one tone to the other to achieve a good legato.

(5) Dynamic level. Each accent should emerge with a *forte* sound when doing this basic technical work. Later on, of course, when applying this approach to musical literature one can modify the fingertip pressure and speed to vary the loudness of an accent.

(6) Shape of hand. After playing an accent the wrist and the fingertip which has just depressed the key will be lower. However, the hand and the fingers must maintain the same shape—the hand cupped and the fingers curved—throughout the process of playing an accent. Otherwise they would be unable to function as a firm unit when transferring the weight and strength of the wrist and forearm to the keys.

(7) Role of elbow and upper arm. The elbow should be kept virtually motionless to prevent the energy from being dissipated and to direct it to the fingertip and the keyboard where the sound will be produced. The upper arm is thus not directly involved when playing an

accent, even when loud chords are involved.

(8) Timing of a series of accents. The performer's wrist moves in a down-up, down-up motion as it goes from note to note. The "down" is the wrist motion which produces the sound; the "up" is the preparation for the next tone. Each complete accent ("down-up" cycle) takes the same time, with half of its duration given to the "down," including the pause which follows it, and half to the "up," including its subsequent pause. There are only two speeds for the motions, a faster one for all of the "downs," and a slower one for all of the "ups." The "up" movement should be a relaxed one since it produces no sound of its own. Its exact velocity is not crucial and may vary from performer to performer, but it should not be too leisurely since one wants to be prepared for the next note sufficiently ahead of time.

The tempo for such a series of accents will vary from person to person. A beginner in this technique may need one-and-a-half to two or more seconds for each down-up cycle, whereas others will need less.

It is often helpful for beginners to count "down, and, up, and; down, and, up, and..." with each syllable receiving an equal amount of time. They should not move on the "and" and should make certain that they are completely relaxed at that moment while maintaining only the minimum pressure needed to keep the finger on the key and to hold the hand position. (I am uncertain whether this approach to counting was suggested by Vengerova or an assistant.) The point of repose on the "ands" helps the student to relax both physically and mentally. A more advanced pupil probably would omit the "ands," but would maintain the instant without motion at both top and bottom.

It must be noted, however, that the essential points in playing an accent are (1) to be prepared on the key beforehand, (2) to play the accent properly, (3) and then to relax. The timing of the motions between accents, when no sound is being produced, is secondary in importance. I have described what is probably the most usual way to do it, but variations can exist which still remain within the framework of the Vengerova system.[14]

[14]Vengerova demonstrated her tolerance in this matter when I asked her which of two different ways to play the accents was correct. Another pupil had shown me that he divided the "up" motion into two parts, an initial one in which the hand returns to the normal level, and a second one made just before playing the next note, which raises the wrist to the height needed to play the accent. Vengerova's assistant, Mildred Jones, heartily disapproved of this procedure, but Vengerova herself said that both the single and double preparation were correct.

I prefer the simplicity of the single "up" motion described in the body of the text. The Vengerova system has enough motions built into it without adding unnecessarily to their number. I also like to be completely prepared for the new note as long in advance as possible.

Indeed, when applying this technique to the performance of music, differences in timing of the movements in between the accents will constantly appear. This rhythm $\frac{4}{4}$ 𝅘𝅥 𝅘𝅥 𝅘𝅥 𝅘𝅥 | must be performed differently from this one $\frac{6}{4}$ 𝅗𝅥 𝅘𝅥 𝅗𝅥 𝅘𝅥 𝅗𝅥 | .

When this five finger exercise is expanded into an eight-note scale pattern, the thumb must pass gradually under the other fingers. This permits the thumb to approximate in slow practice what happens in fast playing when speed requires the thumb motion to be spread over a series of pitches.

Let me illustrate this with a C major scale played by the right hand. After the second finger plays its accent on D the thumb must move underneath it. It passes under the third finger when E is played and moves to F to prepare to play that note. In other words, the thumb keeps up with the other fingers, or is even a shade ahead, as is necessary for it to be ready to play. The wrist should not turn to help the thumb. If it did, the motion would have to be repeated twice in an octave, or eight times in four octaves, which would make it impossible to develop speed in scale playing.[15]

When F is played, the thumb must produce its accent from a position underneath the third finger, and the second finger must then move to G carrying the other fingers along. These should not be two separate motions, but instead a single, unified one. The second finger must start quickly while the thumb is descending on the accent. This is done rapidly even in slow tempo to avoid wasted motion. The thumb, of course, may have to pivot (turn) somewhat on the note to permit this.

A parallel can be made to the motions of divers who twist while falling into the water. They do not fall first and then twist, since it would then be too late and they would already be immersed. Instead they perform the motions simultaneously. In the same way pianists combine into a unified movement the accent on the thumb and the preparation of the second finger. The same approach is followed when playing a

---

[15]Mrs. Snyder and I differ about a detail regarding the passing of the thumb. She holds that in "ones" the third finger must pivot (turn) slightly to the right while playing, to permit the thumb to reach the F, since most pianists cannot get to it comfortably otherwise. (It becomes even more essential for the fourth finger to do this when one later passes the thumb under it.) However, she keeps the fingers in a straight line with the keys when playing "ones" and "twos," whereas I start with them pointing inwards at a slight angle to the keys as would be done in fast playing. (See p. 26.) This makes it easier to pass the thumb without the need for the extra pivoting motions on the third and fourth fingers.

I believe that Vengerova was not concerned about such minor procedural differences, since they did not affect the principles of tone production basic to her system of accents.

descending scale; the accent on the thumb and the preparation of the finger that follows must be combined into one motion.

The reasons for insisting on this procedure become apparent if one imagines having to play a scale in a fast piece with an accent on the thumb but not on any other notes. There would be no time for two motions—one for the accent and one to prepare the new note.

In order to build the habits needed for fast playing, Vengerova insisted that slow practice approximate the conditions existing in a faster tempo. Her system of practicing with accents may seem to contradict this principle; after all, one doesn't usually play with so many accents. However, as will be seen shortly, she had a systematic way of eliminating the unwanted ones so that bad habits would not arise.

When playing scales, with or without accents, the arm should move along freely following the pitch pattern of the scale. The fingers should point inward and at a slight angle to the keys. This is particularly important in fast tempo. (See photo 5, p. 18.) The hand also should not tilt much, if at all, toward the fifth finger. These two aspects of good hand position make it easier both to pass the thumb under and, when going in the reverse direction, to cross the other fingers over the thumb.

C. Accents in "Twos," "Threes," "Fours," and "Eights"

The pitch pattern for practicing with accents.

After the scale has been played by each hand alone for one octave with an accent on each note—"ones" are usually played hands separately only—the scale is now played, first separately and then together, accenting every other note ("twos"). This is done for two octaves so that each pitch of the scale receives an accent and the scale begins and ends with an accent. In "twos" the "down" and "up" portions of the accent cycle now occur over two notes, with the "down" accented and the "up," which still functions as the preparation, unaccented.

It is important to remember to relax immediately after the drop, and to sense as the wrist moves upward that the arm weight is being transferred from the fingertip that has just played to the one about to play.

It is hard to say in print exactly how loud the accented tone should be. Perhaps one could say that it should be *forte,* and the unaccented one *mezzo forte* but still firm in sound. Vengerova herself never described it in such terms but merely stated that all tones were *forte* with some accented and some not.

After playing the scale in "twos" hands separately, one plays it together making certain that both hands use the same motions. In particular, the wrists must reach the same depth and height, and the fingertips must be prepared on the keys before playing. Once it has been learned by the student, this coordination can be applied to pieces to avoid the frequent problem, which Vengerova despised, of not playing with hands together.

After playing "twos" one would play a scale for three octaves, first separately and then together, in "threes." Again, each pitch will receive an accent, although only every third note is accented. Accompanying each accent will now be two unaccented notes. The upward movement should be continuous between them without any point of rest destroying the smoothness of the upward motion. Performers must be careful not to raise the wrist too much on the first note after the accent or they will be unable to raise farther on the following note without reaching an absurdly high level and losing the shape of the hand.

The tempo may be noticeably faster for "threes" than it was for "ones" or "twos," particularly the former, since "twos" can proceed slightly more quickly than "ones." However, the amount by which the tempo increases cannot be described by a formula. In addition, one cannot give a metronome mark for practicing in "ones" or "twos" or for any stage in the series. An advanced player could take a faster tempo than a novice and still maintain proper control.

Next, the scale is played for four octaves, accenting every fourth note ("fours"), beginning and ending with an accent, playing hands separately at first and then together. The tempo will be still faster, though one can, and often does, practice it more slowly to acquire the needed facility.

The last step will be to play the scale with an accent occurring only every eight notes ("eights"). (It is unnecessary to play scales in "fives," "sixes," or "sevens.") It is most convenient to play the scale for only four octaves, as in "fours," so the accents now occur in an ascending major scale on do, re, mi, and fa, and in a descending one on fa, mi, re, do. The top note will be unaccented.

"Eights" can be performed at a fast tempo. The combination of greater speed and fewer accents makes playing in "eights" resemble more closely what is usually associated with scale practicing.

After the accent, if the wrist started to rise immediately on the second note of the eight note group, it might well become uncomfortably high by the seventh or eighth note. To avoid this problem Vengerova suggested that the wrist could remain low, if desired, for the first three notes after the accent, and only start to rise with the fifth note of the eight-note group.

Because the tempo gets faster as one progresses from "ones" to "eights," the depth and height of the wrist movement must be reduced since there is not enough time to make as deep an accent. However, some of the vertical motion must be maintained or stiffness will result, and the sound produced by the quick downward motion of an accent, even if it is not as deep as in "ones," must be preserved. It is essential, too, that the pianist continue to transfer the arm weight from one finger to the next so as to play with a solid sound—sometimes described as "in the keys."

Of course, most students do not proceed from "ones" to "eights" in a single easy lesson. They may have to linger at a particular stage for a while, perhaps playing hands separately at first, until the teacher judges that they are ready to advance to the next level.

It is unnecessary to go through the entire series of accents ("ones," "twos," "threes," "fours," and "eights") for each scale. One would never get done practicing if it were. A student is taught to play a series of scales in "fours" only, and later, when more proficient, in "eights," proceeding chromatically from one to the next. For instance, utilizing "eights" for all of them, one would play C major, then D^b major, then D major, etc.

However, students should go through the entire series of accents daily for several scales to maintain the ability to use these accents properly. Such practice also makes an excellent warm-up exercise.

Practicing in "eights" helps one play an accent wherever desired, is good for legato, and helps avoid stiffness because one keeps a flexible wrist. Since "eights" can be played quite fast, scales also increase in velocity and ease of execution.

Vengerova had no regulation against playing scales at a fast tempo without accents as most advanced painists do. This sort of practice may be needed to play, for example, fast cadenza-like scales, such as often occur in the literature. However, the emphasis in the training of a Vengerova student, at least in the earlier stages, was on practicing technique with accents.

D. Justification for Practicing with Accents

What is to be gained from this entire system of practicing with accents? Can a justification be given for its use?

In reply one could summarize its benefits, some of which are already familiar, by saying that practicing with accents helps one acquire:

(1) A systematic approach to practicing each note individually, and then for organizing these notes into larger groups. This procedure can then be applied to the study of sections of pieces.

(2) Evenness of passagework. Practicing with accents helps the fingers acquire independence and strength so they can play with firmness and equality of sound.

(3) Good legato. Transferring the weight from one fingertip to the next when the accents are removed helps achieve this and also aids the evenness of passagework.

(4) Relaxation where needed. Acquiring this in the wrist and forearm helps avoid the stiffness which can cause rhythmic unevenness in passagework.

(5) The ability to play an accent wherever desired in performance.

(6) A technique which lends itself to musical phrasing and control of color and dynamics. This will be described later on.

(7) Good tone quality. This is aided by keeping the fingertips in contact with the keys at all time (non-percussive touch), and by the insistence that one listen carefully to the sound being produced.

Some claim that the concept of a good tone is an illusion, and that what seem to be differences in tone quality actually come about because of differences in such things as balance, evenness of line, pedaling, and articulation. The chief way in which one tone differs from another is in dynamics.[16] However, it is generally agreed that a non-percussive touch is preferable when practical, since the performer has a more accurate control over the resulting dynamic level. In addition, the actual noise of the fingertip hitting the key, which results from a percussive touch, can disturb the tone quality, though this factor is probably more noticeable if one sits closer to the pianist rather than farther away, since the percussive noise will not carry as far as the string tone.

E. Exercises

During my first year of studies, Vengerova gave me a new exercise at each lesson. After checking it the following week, she would then assign another one. These exercises were assigned, among other reasons, to help my adjustment to her system. Unfortunately, I had not yet begun to keep careful records of what was taught, and can remember only one which clearly dates from that period, Exercise 7c (described on p. 71.)

One can get some idea of what they were like by looking at those contained in the collections by Pischna and Tausig, two volumes of which she was very fond. (At one point she also endorsed the *Daily Studies on the Piano* by Joseffy.)[17]

She insisted that all exercises be practiced within the context of the Vengerova technique, and in particular with a flexible wrist. For instance, when I practiced the Tausig exercises as edited by Ehrlich in the Schirmer edition, I was told to ignore the editor's practice instructions with which she disagreed.

Vengerova also insisted that I be aware of what I was trying to accomplish when practicing an exercise, both to make sure that it was a useful one for my goal and to make certain that it was being practiced in the proper way. She also encouraged me to be discriminating in choosing exercises, and not to play all just because they were included in a recommended volume. When I asked her which of the Tausig were best she did not want to take the time to discuss the merits of each and every one, but she did recommend Nos. 7, 16, 22, and 25, and said to omit Nos. 1, 23, and 24. She also showed me how to make up my own

---

[16]For a discussion of this subject see Otto Ortmann, *The Physical Basis of Piano Touch and Tone* (London: Kegan Paul, Trench, Trubner, and Co., Ltd., 1925).

[17]J. Pischna, *Technical Studies for the Piano* (New York: G. Schirmer, 1904); Carl Tausig, *Daily Studies for the Piano,* ed. H. Ehrlich (New York: G. Schirmer, n.d.); Rafael Joseffy, *Daily Studies on the Piano* (New York: E. Schuberth and Co., 1880).

exercises to help overcome particular problems, and encouraged me to modify an existing one if needed to increase its usefulness.

Vengerova's favorite exercises fell into three main categories: one group strengthened the fingers, increased the power and flexibility of the wrist, and helped focus the arm weight into the fingers within a given hand position when practiced within her system of technique. (Some exercises to help new students relax also fall roughly into this category.) Another set developed speed and flexibility within a pattern that changed hand position, such as a thumb passing exercise for playing scales. (See pp. 34-36 and 54-55 for examples.) The third group, consisting of trill exercises, will be described on p. 64.

Here are three exercises she gave to me, all from the first category, which I still practice frequently as warm-up exercises:

Exercise 3a. Left hand two octaves lower.

Exercise 3a: Play a scale hands separately, dropping on each note in "ones," using the same finger for an octave. Any finger may be used or any pair of adjacent fingers when playing in thirds. (I usually do it first with 4-5, then 3-4, then 2-3, and then 1-2.) Repeat the exercise in different keys ascending chromatically. It is excellent for developing the coordination between the fingertip and the wrist and also, when played in thirds, for developing the strength of the fingers in particular hand positions. However, caution must be observed. To avoid straining the wrist, alternate hands and practice it only briefly.

Exercise 3b.

31

Exercise 3b: Again be careful not to hurt the wrist. Vengerova also suggested practicing it with the accents reversed, so that the accent was played by the fourth finger each time. But since this strained my fourth finger, I avoided doing it that way.

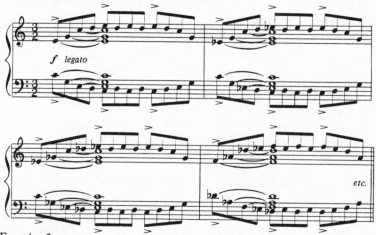

Exercise 3c.

Exercise 3c: This needs no special description.

Here are three exercises to help new students relax. When I returned to Vengerova after an absence of about a year and a half, her assistant Mildred Jones taught me Exercise 3d. She also gave me Exercise 3e, but since I cannot find it described in my notes, I am giving what may be a slightly different version that another assistant, Mrs. Snyder, showed me (along with Exercise 3f) while I was writing this book. *All three should be done hands separately only.*

Exercise 3d.

Exercise 3d: Drop with the wrist, with the fingers prepared on the keys beforehand, as if playing accents in ones on each chord, but with a slow descent and a soft sound. This helps you sense in an easy and relaxed manner the various hand positions of a scale. The exact number of octaves to be played is flexible. Transpose this exercise to other keys, placing the groups of notes according to the normal scale fingering of each key.

32

Exercise 3e.

Exercise 3e: Let a firm hand and fingers fall freely on the notes from at least two inches above the key while also dropping the wrist. Use only the natural weight of the hand. This determines the appropriate degree of loudness which varies from individual to individual, since the weight does also. After relaxing the hand for a second or two on the notes, flatten the fingers and slide the hand off the keyboard with completely relaxed dead weight. (Sit near the edge of the chair and far enough away from the piano to allow the arm to slide comfortably all of the way down.) Feel the relaxation from the hand to the shoulder. This exercise may also be transposed to other keys beginning on white notes.

Exercise 3f. Left hand two octaves lower.

Exercise 3f ("Every note with a big swing"): This is done in any key beginning on a white note, with the fingers placed on adjacent notes. Play an accent on each finger dropping the wrist in its usual manner while maintaining the curved shape of the finger. Make a soft sound, however, falling percussively from above, though the finger should be over its key beforehand. Avoid unnecessary tension at all times. Take about ten seconds to play each note while counting "One, and, two, and, three, and, four, and." Begin lifting the wrist on the "and" after the third count and disconnect the finger on the "and" after the fourth count. The lifting of the wrist causes the disconnection. Play the next note on the following count of "One."

This exercise can also be played legato and with a non-percussive sound produced by starting each tone on the surface of the key rather than from above.

It appears to me that the essential features of this exercise are the method of tone production in *piano* and the relaxation that should be present at all times. The timing of the lifting of the wrist is secondary in importance and probably could be modified. Those who do it with ease can also take a somewhat faster tempo provided they do not lose the relaxation.

33

F. Further Observations on Practicing Scales

Vengerova had her students practice scales in the major, harmonic, and melodic minor forms using standard fingerings, with the hands separated at the intervals of the octave, third, sixth, and tenth. She did not assign scales in contrary motion.

She and her assistants also had various supplementary exercises for scale practice (Exercises 3g to 3o) to help with problems associated with passing the thumb under, or with crossing the other fingers over the thumb, since practicing with accents did not guarantee that these difficulties would be solved.

Exercises 3g-m.

(3n)

(3o)

Exercises 3n and 3o.

Please note the following about these exercises:

(1) They can be done in any order desired.

(2) They can be transposed to all keys, major and minor, with the fingering and pitch pattern adjusted to the placement of the thumb in that key. Exercise 3i, written in E^b major, shows how this is done.

Exercise 3i adapted to E^b major for the right hand.

(If transposed exactly, the E^b major fingering would require beginning with the third finger on A^b, thus defeating the purpose of the exercise.)

(3) It is not necessary to practice all of the exercises.

(4) Exercises 3g-k may each be repeated as often as needed without stopping.

(5) They are to be played hands separately.

(6) The thumb must pass under the other fingers gradually without the aid of lateral motions of the wrist. (See p. 25.)

(7) Where accents are marked they are to be made in the usual Vengerova fashion.

(8) For Exercises 3n and 3o please note the following:

(a)They should be played for four octaves. This can also be done for Exercises 3L and 3m.

(b) Since the same fingers do not land on the same scale steps in all keys, it is important to remember that in 3n the long note always comes on the thumb, and in 3o on the pitch after the thumb.

35

(c) They are difficult to notate rhythmically. The short notes should be played almost like grace notes but still must be clearly articulated.

(d) The wrist drops on the long notes but without making an accent, or at least not a big one. (The entire dynamic level was not more than *mezzo piano,* or at most *mezzo forte.*) The wrist rises on the short notes.

(e) Vengerova emphasized the importance of these exercises and required that they be practiced in all keys, progressing chromatically from one to the next. She assigned them early in my studies—Exercise 3n one week and Exercise 3o the next.

(f) When playing 3n the note after the thumb must be prepared as soon as possible. When playing 3o one must arrive quickly on the note after the thumb without any wasted motion.

Mildred Jones showed me that 3o can be modified to develop speed in scales after the student's technique has matured (Exercise 3p).

Exercise 3p.

As an aid to the passing of the thumb Vengerova gave me Exercise 3q—a scale played hands separately for two octaves in "fours," using the same fingering over and over again (1-2-3-4, 1-2-3-4, etc.) instead of the usual one. The scale would be transposed upward chromatically, again using the same fingering.

Exercise 3q.

36

Zadel Skolovsky expanded and modified this approach to the practice of the passing of the thumb. He suggested playing scales hands separately without accents as follows:

2 octaves, using only 1-2 continuously repeated.

3 octaves, using only 1-2-3 continuously repeated.

4 octaves, using 1-2-3-4 continuously repeated.

5 octaves, using 1-2-3-4-5 continuously repeated.

One should also see Exercise 7c on p. 71 which helps develop the curvature of the thumb's first joint that is needed for playing scales.

Mrs. Snyder recommended playing a scale for two octaves hands separately at an even pace in a moderate tempo before practicing it with accents or doing any of these exercises. This orients the student to the pattern of the key and the physical motions required, and thus makes the work easier.

G. Applying the Technique to Music

The Vengerova system can be applied to all kinds of music and not just to passagework in running sixteenth-notes or to pieces with many sharp accents. An analysis of the the exact motion involved for a particular passage, however, can be misleading if the resulting sound is not heard. While some phrases tend to be played only in certain basic ways, others might vary according to the person's touch, build, weight, hand size, etc. This is one area where only a live demonstration or possibly a sound film would work satisfactorily.

Initially students must think carefully about the system's application to literature. Gradually it becomes easier and more comfortable for them to use, until eventually it should feel perfectly normal and natural.

Three examples will be given now of the method's application. Others will appear later in different contexts.

(1) The melodic accent of a melody—the note receiving the greatest emphasis—is played with a drop of the wrist similar to an accent in scales. However, for a tone softer than *forte,* the fingertip pressure and the speed of the wrist motion must be reduced and adjusted to produce the desired dynamic level. The fingertip and hand must remain firm at all times regardless of such modifications.

The wrist usually rises gradually between melodic accents to prepare for the following drop, and one transfers the weight from one fingertip to the next. But these principles cannot be applied mechanically. Often, because of the rhythmic pattern and the layout of the passage, it will be more comfortable if the wrist rises at an uneven pace, and does not reach the same height at all times.

(2) To perform a short crescendo leading to an accent, the wrist should be raised gradually during the crescendo while increasing note by note the amount of weight being shifted into the fingertips. The upward motion culminates with a drop of the wrist on the musical accent.

(3) While the hand normally remains level when playing an accent, and does not tilt to the right or left, exceptions do occur. For instance, in the finale to the Schumann Piano Concerto (Example 3-1) Vengerova told me to prepare the accent desired on the B in the right hand at the downbeat of bar 145 by tilting to the right. This helps to bring the power of the rotary muscles into play and to produce the accent more easily in this passage. (Photos 7 and 8, p. 18, although for a different piece and problem, apply surprisingly well here. Photo 7 shows the incorrect way, photo 8 the correct.)

Example 3-1. Schumann, Piano Concerto in A Minor, Op. 54, third movement, measures 144-47. Vengerova's pedaling is included.

H. The Hand Following the Fingers

An important principle of Vengerova's theory was that the hand should follow the fingers so that the weight is transferred from one fingertip to the next. Example 3-2 from the Chopin Etude Op. 10, No. 5 ("Black Key") illustrates this. Between the first and the fourth sixteenth-notes the wrist and the hand will swing somewhat to the right, thus shifting the weight in that direction also, and into the fourth finger which might otherwise sound weaker than the rest. This was a major way that Vengerova's pupils achieved an even sound.

Example 3-2. Chopin, Etude Op. 10, No. 5, "Black Key," (Leipzig: Kistner, 1833), measures 3-4. (The fingering, which is not original, shows what I used.)

Another interesting feature of this example is that the motion of the hand helps the thumb move from the initial D^b to the A^b four notes later. This type of movement would be inappropriate when passing the thumb under in scales, for there the thumb and wrist must move continuously and evenly, whereas here the pattern permits them to pause briefly on the A^bs and E^bs. These motions should be repeated for each successive beat. Simultaneously the arm should move gradually and smoothly to the right in the course of these two bars.

The left hand figuration from Chopin's *Fantasie-Impromptu* (Example 3-3) provides another illustration of how the hand (and other parts of the body) follow the fingers. Here the wrist will swing freely to the right as the musical figure approaches the thumb, and then back to the left when it returns to the fifth finger.

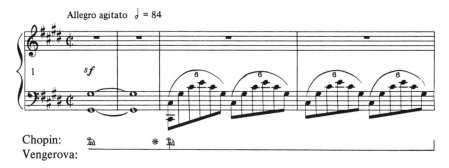

Example 3-3. Chopin, *Fantaisie-Impromptu*, Op. 66 (Berlin: A.M. Schlesinger, 1855), measures 1-4.

One other point should be made about this common accompaniment pattern, frequently found in Chopin. The pitch pattern first ascends, then descends, and then repeats itself more or less intact, with a majority of the same notes being found in the descent as in the ascent. Rather than have the wrist move to the right and then return in the same plane, it is better to have it make some sort of circular motion so that it can move continuously and not have to stop at the end of each pattern. (Actually the movement will look more like an ellipse than a circle.) One can start with the wrist moving at a low level to the right, rising on the thumb, returning high to the left, and then falling on the fifth finger to repeat the processs. This will give a counterclockwise circle. The reverse direction is also possible: one can start moving high to the right, fall on the thumb, return to the left at a low wrist level, and then rise on the fifth finger to repeat the process. An emphasis can be given to the bass note either way, even though in one pattern the fifth finger moves downward and in the other one upward. One can also fall on the thumb if desired without making an accent. One chooses whether to move clockwise or counterclockwise according to what feels most comfortable and will coordinate better with the other hand.

Chapter IV

Etudes

Vengerova considered the study of etudes essential to the development of her students' technique. Generally her pupils worked on one in addition to technical material (scales, exercises, arpeggios, etc.) and other pieces, unless one of the latter was etude-like.

For instance, in my first years with her I was assigned selections from Op. 740 of Czerny, the *Gradus ad Parnassum* of Clementi (Tausig edition), and the Moszkowski Etudes, Op. 72. Gradually through the years other studies were introduced: the Mendelssohn Etudes, Op. 104; various ones by Chopin; the *Perpetual Motion* of Weber; Moszkowski's *En Automne,* Op. 36, No. 4, and Etude in G^b, Op. 24, No. 1 (both rather Lisztian in technique); and Liszt's *Un Sospiro, Waldesrauschen,* and No. 6 of the Paganini-Liszt's series.

When assigning studies from the volumes by Clementi, Czerny, and Moszkowski (Op. 72) mentioned above, Vengerova preferred perpetual-motion etudes featuring varieties of scale and arpeggio patterns. She avoided pieces with more than a single repeated note in the basic figuration, or with odd rhythmic patterns (e.g., five notes to a beat), or with staccato notes except in the accompaniment. In addition to studies with single note passagework she assigned etudes containing double notes in one hand.

She specified that etudes with a perpetual-motion figuration be practiced and played at a continuous *forte* level disregarding any dynamic or expression markings in the score. The hand with the moving voice—often in a pattern of four sixteenth-notes to a beat—is practiced first in "ones" for one or two bars. (A greater number of bars is unlikely because "ones" and "twos," particularly "ones," are fatiguing, both mentally and physically, and care must be taken not to strain the wrist.) These same bars are then practiced in "twos." After that the next bar or two are practiced in the same way. Then both of these groups of bars are combined, first in "twos" and then in "fours." "Threes" are omitted, unless triplets are present, since they do not fit the rhythmic pattern of the etude. This process is then repeated for another similar number of bars, and then both sets are put together in "fours." The entire composition is learned in this fashion. More advanced students also learn etudes in "eights." The individual sections are learned hands separately first, and then together. It is not necessary to study the entire composition hands separately before putting them together.

If the right hand plays the rhythmic pattern given above and the left hand plays just a single note on each of the beats, as is common in Czerny, the left hand will be in "ones" and the right hand in "fours," since the wrist motions should match. If one of the left hand notes is staccato, it would be played in the usual manner, except that the hand would snap the fingers away from the keys immediately after playing the note and before preparing the next one. (Also see section (1c) on p. 66.)

Here are two other examples of how the Vengerova system of practicing was adjusted to the metric and rhythmic structure of the music:

(1) If one practices an etude which has six sixteenth-notes to a beat, e.g., $\frac{2}{4}$ ♪♪♪♪♪♪♪♪♪♪♪♪ | , one uses "ones," "twos," and "threes," omits "fours" and "eights," and plays in "sixes," even though that pattern is not otherwise used.

(2) The Czerny etude, Op. 740, No. 37, which has this rhythmic pattern $\frac{3}{8}$ ♪♪♪♪♪♪♪♪♪ | , is performed with one accent to the bar in "nines."

It is usually unnecessary when practicing an etude to reverse the accents. When playing passagework with four sixteenth-notes to a beat, the first note of each beat should receive an accent whether one is practicing in "ones," "twos," or "fours." Starting a series of accents on the second sixteenth or the third sixteenth, etc. ("reverse accents"), could disturb one's sense of the rhythmic organization of the work.

Her assistant, Zadel Skolovsky, however, showed me how an individual passage could be practiced hands separately this way to help acquire evenness and control. Vengerova also emphasized its usefulness to Lilian Kallir who employs it as an everyday tool. My own experience, though, led me to use it more sparingly, and only when other practice techniques did not work.

Normal accents in "twos"

Normal accents in "fours"

"Reverse accents" in "twos"

"Reverse accents" in "fours"
—three possible ways

On successive days of practice one need not repeat all that was previously done. One can begin immediately in "fours," although if a passage gives trouble one might have to resort to "ones" and "twos," or even to "reverse accents." Any bar which does not work well can be practiced out of context.

It should be noted that practicing etudes in accents without musical shadings was an exception to Vengerova's usual insistence that the notes and the musical markings be learned at the same time.

Often a student would feel that a point of repose would be helpful when practicing a work in "fours" or "eights." Vengerova suggested that one could accomplish this by practicing a bar or more using one of the following rhythmic transformations which stop after the accent:

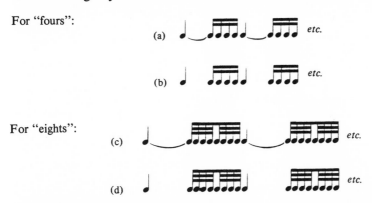

The notation given above is only approximate, since the relationship of the short notes to the long one (accents) was not rigidly fixed. In (b) and (d) the first short note after the accent repeats the pitch of the accented note although it was not notated this way in the etude.

This rhythmic approach to practicing can be used to help acquire speed and fluency in passagework, in pieces as well as etudes. Vengerova first showed this to me in the C minor section of the finale of the Beethoven Sonata in E^b, Op. 7 (Example 4-1). Since she found that practicing with accents alone did not give me the needed ease and speed, she suggested that working with the above patterns might help.

43

Example 4-1. Beethoven, Sonata in E^b Major, Op. 7, fourth movement, measures 64-65.

It was sufficient to play a Czerny etude at a good tempo with a solid *forte* sound in accents of "fours" or "eights," without musical expression. But with works of greater musical value—e.g., the Moszkowski Etudes, Op. 72, and, of course, Chopin etudes—one would also want to perform the piece with suitable shadings and proper phrasing. The transition from practicing in accents is surprisingly easy to make. One obviously must modify the dynamics and eliminate most accents, but one maintains the lightness and flexibility of the wrist to help avoid stiffness and to help transfer the weight to make *crescendi* and *diminuendi.* It is amazing how the passagework often seems to ripple effortlessly at this stage. This same approach to practicing can apply to works other than etudes, or to sections of larger works, which contain lots of running notes. It often pays to practice them for a while with accents and without expression, and afterward to put in the musical shadings.

When playing an etude or an etude-like passage musically, the spacing of the wrist drops will usually vary. If a 4/4 measure with running sixteenth-notes needs an accent on every beat, it should be played in "fours." If the next bar requires only two accents, spaced evenly in the bar, it should be performed in "eights." The following bar might need only one accent, and so one might say that it is played in "sixteens." The technique should be adapted to serve the needs of the music.

To play a legato passage elegantly and evenly without overemphasizing each note, have the rising wrist play the notes instead of the fingers. Although this instruction is not literally true since the fingers must still do some work, thinking of it this way keeps them from straining and overarticulating.

Etudes of a Lisztian type were more complicated to practice since many types of melodic lines are interwoven with the passagework. While some individual sections could be practiced intitially in the above manner, that is, with accents and without dynamic shading and

44

expression, this approach would not fit much of the music. From the very beginning it took considerable technical and musical insight to know how to work on such pieces. Because of their greater complexity, there was no convenient formula for practicing them as there was with perpetual-motion etudes.

Vengerova helped her students to build up the endurance and speed needed for extended virtuoso works by assigning many etudes. Furthermore, this helped them to cope, both physically and mentally, with a great variety of technical problems.

Chapter V

Singing Tone

(1) When she had to play a single line melody with a lyric, nocturne-like sound, Vengerova did not bother to maintain the neat, carefully controlled hand position which was described initially. In the opening of the Chopin F Minor Nocturne (Example 5-1), for instance, she wanted the melody to sing with a sound that was full, but not overly large, since the dynamic marking is only *piano*. She would still drop on a melodic accent but in a far more leisurely manner, and if her fingers were flatter than usual, or her thumb came off the keyboard when it was not playing, that did not matter. (See photo 6, p. 18.) What was important was that the weight flowed from one tone to the next because the hand and finger remained firm and transferred the arm weight into the keys.

Example 5-1. Chopin, Nocturne in F Minor, Op. 55, No. 1 (Leipzig: Breitkopf und Härtel, 1844), measures 1-5.

(2) Different problems arise when one must bring out a particular note in a chord. Most commonly it will be played by the third, fourth, or fifth finger—the soprano in the right hand or the bass in the left hand. Let us assume that the fifth finger must sing. Vengerova would tilt the hand toward that finger, making it lower than the rest of the hand so that more weight goes into the fifth finger. (This hand position would not be permitted in scale playing, which has a different set of technical problems.) The same principle applies regardless of whether one plays with a downward or upward wrist movement. To bring out a note in a chord with the thumb or second finger, she would also tilt the hand

toward that finger. The direction of the tilt is now reversed from that used to bring out the fifth finger.

In the beginning of this Schubert slow movement (Example 5-2) both hands have the melody simultaneously. The right hand must tilt toward the fifth finger, the left hand toward the thumb. (On p. 18 photo 7 shows the incorrect position for the right hand, photo 8 the correct.)

Example 5-2. Schubert, Sonata in A Major, Op. 120, D.V. 664, second movement, measures 1-5.

(a) Although Vengerova never described it this way, it should be mentioned that it is easier for some pianists to tilt toward the fifth finger if the elbow is close to the body, and it is easier to tilt toward the thumb if the elbow is away from the body.

(b) This tilting (turning, leaning) of the hand is one form of "rotation" in the terminology of Tobias Matthay, the English pedagogue. (Vengerova never used that word, incidentally.) In this case rotation involves a simple turning of the rotary muscles and not a vibratory (rocking back and forth) movement.

(c) Vengerova also said that one could swing the wrist—either from left to right, or right to left—in addition to tilting, to help get the weight into the melody note. She emphasized that one must experiment to find the most suitable solutions to the needs of the particular passage.

(3) She also suggested practicing scales in "ones" with a singing tone–in this case not with the usual *forte* accent, but with one produced by a slower descent of a firm wrist—to help each finger acquire the ability to produce a warm rich sound.

(4) While Vengerova usually emphasized the importance of making the melodic line sing, when I played this passage from Debussy's "La soirée dans Grenade" (Example 5-3), she remarked that the style of impressionist music generally requires the middle voices to sound richer in relationship to the melody than would be the case in Romantic music, for example. The transparency of sonority appropriate to the impressionists must be maintained, however.

47

Example 5-3. Debussy, "La soirée dans Grenade," measures 23-26.

Chapter VI

Arpeggios, Double Notes, Leaps, and Trills

A. Arpeggios

Vengerova had her students practice arpeggios in major and minor triads and in dominant and diminished seventh forms. She usually did not assign other patterns, although she did tell me when I was studying the finale of the Schumann Piano Concerto to work on the somewhat unusual forms that occur there as I would on a triad or dominant seventh arpeggio.

Her fingerings were traditional, and were based on the following principles according to my analysis:

(1) In the right hand play the thumb as soon as possible; in the left hand as late as possible. (Arpeggios are begun ascending.)

(2) Avoid putting the thumb on a black key with the necessary exceptions of triad arpeggios in E^b minor and F# major.

(3) Substitute the second finger where appropriate for another at the start of a right-hand arpeggio, or at the top of a left-hand one.

(4) To decide whether to use the third or fourth finger in a triad arpeggio, study the procedures given below which are based on the standard fingerings for four-note chords using the fifth finger. These chords are found in broken form in the left hand in the bass, and in the right hand in the treble, for arpeggio positions beginning on the white keys, plus all positions in E^b minor and F# major. The fingering for the remaining positions should be derived from the most closely related forms. (Exceptions occur in Vengerova's fingerings only in E^b minor, right hand, second inversion, and in F# major, left hand, root position.)

(a) Use the fourth finger if the note in question is closer to the fifth finger than to the second:

(b) Use the third finger if the note in question is closer to the second than to the fifth:

(c) Use the fourth finger if the note in question is equidistant on the keyboard between the second and fifth fingers:

Arpeggios with identical fingering and hand position are grouped together. Practicing only one of them is sufficient to learn all.

Below is an illustration of the fingering for a **D Major** arpeggio written out for the usual four octaves:

root position

first inversion

second inversion

50

Fingerings for Triad Arpeggios

(Major keys are indicated by capital letters; minor keys by lower case letters. Vengerova allowed the exceptional fingerings in parentheses, but preferred the others.)

		uninv	1st inv	2nd inv
C, d, e, F, G, a	R.H.	1231	1241	1241
	L.H.	5421	5421	5321
D, E, A	R.H.	1231	2124	1241
	L.H.	5321	3213	5321
		(4)	(4) (4)	
c, f, g	R.H.	1231	2123	1231
	L.H.	5421	4214	5321
D^b, E^b, A^b	R.H.	2124	1241	2412
	L.H.	2142	5421	4214
c#, f#, g#	R.H.	2124	1241	2412
	L.H.	2142	5421	4214
B^b	R.H.	2124	1241	1241
	L.H.	3213	5421	5321
b^b	R.H.	2312	2123	1231
	L.H.	3213	2132	5321
B	R.H.	1231	2312	2123
	L.H.	5321	3213	2132
b	R.H.	1231	1241	2123
	L.H.	5421	5421	4214
e^b	R.H.	1231	1241	1241
	L.H.	5421	5421	5321
F#	R.H.	1231	1241	1241
	L.H.	5421	5421	5321

In addition to requiring that triad arpeggios be played with hands an octave apart, Vengerova also had us practice them in other starting positions. The initial distance between the hands varies from a fifth to an eleventh in these nine possible combinations.

Starting positions for practicing triad arpeggios.

Fingerings for Dominant Seventh Arpeggios

(These were given to me by Vengerova's assistant, Mildred Jones. The fingerings in italics are exceptions to the basic principles, but make the arpeggios easier to play.)

		univ	1st inv	2nd inv	3rd inv
C (spelled: GBDF)	R.H.	1234	1234	1234	1234
	L.H.	5432	5432	5432	5432
G, D, A	R.H.	1234	2123	1234	1234
	L.H.	5432	4321	5432	5432
E	R.H.	1234	2312	2123	1234
	L.H.	5432	4321	3214	5432
B	R.H.	2341	2312	2123	1234
	L.H.	4321	3214	2143	5432
F#	R.H.	2123	1234	*2341*	1234
	L.H.	*2143*	5432	4321	5432
D^b, A^b	R.H.	2123	1234	2341	2312
	L.H.	2143	5432	4321	3214
E^b	R.H.	2123	1234	1234	2312
	L.H.	3214	5432	5432	4321
B^b, F	R.H.	1234	1234	1234	2123
	L.H.	5432	5432	5432	4321

Diminished seventh arpeggios are fingered and played according to the same principles as triad and dominant seventh arpeggios.

52

It would be well now to analyze in some detail what happens when one plays an arpeggio. The procedures that follow were taught to me by Vengerova as corrections when I was having trouble with an arpeggio in a composition. Some of her remarks may have been particularly designed to fit the shape of my hand, which may be seen in the photographs, but it is hoped that most will apply to other pianists, too.

Let us imagine that you are playing an ascending uninverted C major triad arpeggio with the right hand, starting with the C on the bass staff. (The principles learned from this arpeggio will apply to others.) Hold the hand level initially as in scale playing but with the fingers spread apart. (See photo 9, p. 19.) After you play the first note with the thumb, move it gradually under the second and third fingers as you play them, so that the thumb will be ready for the next C. Keep the third finger in contact with its key until you play the thumb to ensure a good legato. (See photos 10-12, p. 19. They will also apply to a descending arpeggio when playing G).

During this process you are moving the arm to the right, causing the second and third fingers to flatten somewhat after they are played and to lose the curved position they initially held. As soon as you play the third finger, move the second finger close to it, thereby helping you move the hand in the direction of the arpeggio. Keep the forearm and wrist at the same angle to the keyboard throughout a long arpeggio, at least until an extreme register of the piano. Any appreciable motion at the inside (thumb side) of the wrist could result in a serious loss of speed. When you play the thumb after the third finger, it may be momentarily on the back of the nail, or part of it, but this will last only an instant until it pivots to permit you to move the second finger to E, with the entire process then repeating itself in the next octave.

The situation is reversed for a descending right hand C major arpeggio. When you play the thumb on C at the end of the first octave, let it pivot to help cross the hand over it as you move the third finger towards its next note. The third and second fingers should be close to each other and flat at this point. (See photos 10-12, p. 19.) If curved beforehand they would be too near the edge of the white keys. You would then have to slide them toward the black keys, which is an extra motion causing a loss of speed, or it will be difficult to make the thumb reach the keyboard without forcing the second and third fingers into an awkward, overcurved position.

You need not straighten out the hand to facilitate the thumb reach. To do so would result in a sharp turn at the inside of the wrist, which would slow you down. Moving the arm to the left, and increasing the

53

curvature of the third and second fingers after you play them—the arm movement helps bring this about—along with a little effort to make the thumb find its new note, will suffice. The arm movement also will help you move the second finger to its note from its position close to the third finger.

I hope that this brief description of what happens in arpeggio playing will be helpful. A word of caution is in order, though, for teachers who use this material: these ideas should be introduced only gradually and as needed. Students should be permitted to solve some of theses difficulties on their own, so that they do not become inhibited and confused by the sheer number of points to be remembered beforehand.

Arpeggios, too, can profit from systematic work with accents. I cannot recall, however, at what stage in the development of my arpeggio technique that Vengerova first required me to use them. It may be preferable initially to teach arpeggios without accents and to add them later on. At the beginning students have enough trouble with the motions of the arpeggios themselves without imposing extra ones on them.

Here are some useful exercises Vengerova prescribed for the practice of arpeggios:

Exercise 6a (beginning).

L.H.

Exercise 6a (conclusion).

Exercise 6a, to be done hands separately, can be transposed to any desired pitches. Small hands may not be able to carry the exercise as far as is indicated.

Exercises 6b-c.

Exercises 6b and 6c can each be repeated several times in a row, and can be adapted to fit the pitch and fingering pattern of any arpeggio being studied. When practicing Exercise 6b, as well as any arpeggio in which the thumb is on the beat and therefore easily accented, care must be taken to ensure that the thumb is prepared on the key before playing. Otherwise the key will be slapped and will always be played with an accent, whether or not this is musically desirable.

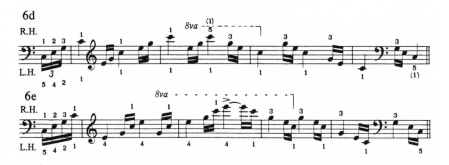

Exercises 6d-e. Left hand an octave lower.

55

Exercises 6d and 6e are helpful rhythmic variants similar to scale preparatory Exercises 3n and 3o on p. 35. Their rhythmic notation as given above is only approximate, for one might want to play the short notes more quickly than is indicated. Note also that in Exercise 6e an extra note (E) has been added in the treble to increase the amount of practice obtained from the pattern. Such modifications can be made freely where desired.

Exercise 6d forces one to get the thumb under quickly. One should then prepare the following finger immediately. Exercise 6e requires that the finger after the thumb be played rapidly and precisely.

Vengerova also suggested making up exercises on dominant seventh chords to help the hands get a better grasp of the positions involved. One must use caution though to ensure that the frequently awkward stretches do not strain a small hand or cause stiffness. Exercise 6f, an example of this type, can be made easier by omitting the initial chord.

Exercise 6f. Left hand two octaves lower.

Exercise 6g also serves this purpose well, although it was originally assigned to help get greater firmness in my fingers when playing the chords at the beginning of the finale to the Schumann Concerto. Its four versions are to be practiced hands separately, the left hand two octaves lower, accenting each note with a drop of the wrist ("ones") except for the sixteenth notes in (d). (The pitch of the chords should be modified successively according to the pattern given at the bottom line of the example.)

Exercise 6g: top two lines. Bottom line: pitch pattern for deriving new chords for the exercise. The starting chord for the series may be transposed.

This is an extremely useful exercise to help grasp any seventh chord firmly, which aids the playing of its arpeggio. It is, however, very strenuous. To avoid injuring the wrist it is helpful to alternate hands, and to do only a small number of the possible versions and chord positions at one time.

It can also be useful to block arpeggios as shown below in Exercise 6h. Blocking a pattern makes a chord or interval out of a group of notes meant to be played separately, When playing quickly, few would prepare both notes simultaneously as the exercise would seem to suggest, but practicing this way helps get a firm grasp of the notes.

Exercise 6h. Left hand two octaves lower.

B. Double Notes

Double thirds

Vengerova had her students practice major and minor scales in double thirds, that is scales played in thirds with both notes in one hand. These would be learned first separately, and then hands together.

There are two basic ways to finger these scales. While Vengerova seemed to prefer one (a) since she used it more often, she also employed the other (b) in a few scales. In both cases the fingering remains the same in all octaves, and does not change when descending. With pattern (a) the fifth finger may be played again in some scales when the left hand begins or the right hand ends.

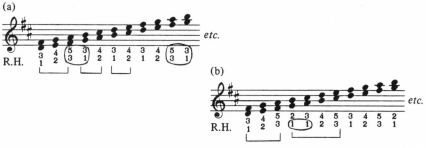

The two ways to finger double thirds.

57

Pattern (a) has the disadvantage of having the third finger played twice in a row (note circles), and also requires three hand positions per octave. This results in more shifting than is demanded by the two hand positions of pattern (b). Pattern (b), however, suffers from having the thumb played consecutively (note circle), as well as from the rather sharp change in hand position produced by playing the second finger immediately after the fifth.

Since the fifth finger plays only once in an octave in pattern (a) and only twice in pattern (b), when giving fingerings for these scales Vengerova would mention only on what pitch(es) the fifth finger plays, and let us fit the others to this.

Fingerings for double thirds. (The tonic is the lower note at the start of each scale.) The fifth finger is on:

Major scales

Scale	l.h.	r.h.	Scale	l.h.	r.h.	Scale	l.h.	r.h.	Scale	l.h.	r.h.
C	a	g	A	a,d	e,b	F#	e#	f#	E^b	c	g
G	c	d	E	a	b	D^b	b^b	g^b	B^b	g	g
D	*g	a	B	a#	f#	A^b	f	g	F	f	e

*Here a is preferable; begin with $\frac{2}{4}$.

Harmonic minor scales

Scale	l.h.	r.h.	Scale	l.h.	r.h.	Scale	l.h.	r.h.	Scale	l.h.	r.h.
C	c	c	A	d	b	F#	a	b,e#	E^b	c^b	d
G	g,c	d,a	E	a	b	C#	a	b#	B^b	b^b	g^b
D	g	e	B	a#	a#	G#	e	fx	F	f	d^b

Vengerova herself gave me the fingering for the harmonic minors. Mildred Jones had earlier given me those for the major scales. For further information on the fingering of all double note scales Vengerova recommended Book II of the *School of Scales and Double Notes for the Piano* by Moritz Moszkowski.[18] This is a fairly extensive compendium of most of the practical fingerings for scales in double notes. Fingerings are given for diatonic scales in thirds (including melodic

[18]London: Enoch & Co., 1901.

minor scales), fourths, and sixths, as well as for all chromatic scales from the interval of a major second up to that of a major sixth. The scales are all written out with clear and unambiguous fingering. Moszkowski's approach is not arbitrary, for he often includes a number of alternative fingerings and lets the individual make the choice.

Book III of this same set, which Madame also endorsed, is a treasurehouse of useful double note exercises, based on a variety of intervals, not just thirds. In most cases Moszkowski takes a basic pattern and moves it systematically through many positions and/or keys, to develop speed, facility, and strength in various hand positions. These exercises are useful, too, as preparation for chordal passages, since control over a variety of interval patterns is an aid in learning to play chords. The very first exercise in Book III (Example 6-1) is typical of Moszkowski's method.

Example 6-1. Moszkowski, *School of Scales and Double Notes for the Piano,* Bk. III, exercise A.1., measures 1-3.

The Pischna and Tausig collections of exercises, both beloved by Madame as mentioned earlier, also include some good double note material.[19]

Scales in double notes should first be practiced hands separately until a reasonable facility has been achieved. Only then should one begin playing them hands together. Above all, one must avoid breaking (rolling) any of the thirds. Practicing with accents helps the fingertips make firm contact with the keys. Each voice should be practiced separately, using the same fingering and legato required when both

[19]J. Pischna, *Technical Studies for the Piano* (New York: G. Schirmer, 1904); Carl Tausig, *Daily Studies for the Piano,* ed. H. Ehrlich (New York: G. Schirmer, n.d.).

voices are played together.[20] At first this may seem awkward, but some of the speed and fluency thus attained should remain when the voices are combined.

When playing these notes in a C major scale, a perfect legato can be achieved at the place circled if the thumb is passed under the second finger and the third finger is crossed over the fourth. I was expected to follow this procedure whenever possible. A careful placement of the fingers so that the third is near the black keys, and the thumb near the front edge of the keyboard makes this more comfortable. The wrist should also be positioned somewhat inward toward the center of the body. (Photo 13, p. 20, shows the fingers prepared to play ♪.)

When playing the same notes in a descending pattern, the second finger is crossed over the thumb and the fourth finger is passed under the third at the place circled.

Along with many other pianists and teachers, Vengerova preferred when playing a chromatic scale in double minor thirds to slide the second finger from black key to white, rather than to slide the thumb from one white note to another. At the points marked with an asterisk she

Fingering for the chromatic scale in double minor thirds.

[20]Alfred Cortot's editions of the Chopin Etudes (*Twelve Studies,* Op. 10, Paris: Editions Salabert, 1915; *Twelve Studies,* Op. 25, Paris: Editions Salabert, 1917) have suggestions on how to develop fluency in playing the individual voices in double notes. These are found in his practice instructions to Op. 10, No. 2, and Op. 25, Nos. 6, 8, and 10. He recommends playing diatonic scales using only a pair of fingers throughout, such as 1-2, 3-4, or 4-5, to help each pair achieve a good legato. (I did each exercise hands separately for two octaves.) Using 3-4 and 4-5 teaches one to cross the longer fingers over the shorter, e.g., 3 over 4, and to pass the shorter fingers under the longer, e.g., 4 under 3. The same exercises played chromatically help with chromatic double notes.

Another useful exercise for chromatic double notes is to practice sliding with each of the fingers from black key to white, for example: ♪ .

Although I never discussed these editions with Vengerova, the exercises worked well with her system of technique and helped my playing of double notes while I was studying with her.

permitted the substitution of the fifth finger for the fourth if preferred.

Legato octaves

In order to play legato octaves one chooses a legato fingering for the outer voices if one's hand is big enough—e.g., 4-5, or 3-4-5, rather than 5-5-5. Some of the same techniques used for playing legato double thirds would then apply, such as crossing longer fingers over shorter ones, and passing shorter fingers under longer.

When I played the Chopin Polonaise in C Minor (Example 6-2), the correct management of the thumb, which must play continuously in the legato octave passages, gave me trouble. Either Vengerova or an assistant told me the following about how to handle the problem:

Example 6-2. Chopin, Polonaise in C Minor, Op. 40, No. 2 (Leipzig: Breitkopf und Härtel, 1840), measures 1-5.

A legato outer voice can mask a non-legato thumb, but it is better if both voices are connected. To play the thumb legato in scale passages on the white keys, slide the thumb to the edge of the next key after playing a note, and hold the first note to the last possible moment before playing the next one. In addition, graze the thumb along the surface of the keys without ever raising it above them. These techniques will permit you to connect the two notes with a minimum of break. To develop this facility, practice scales this way with the thumb alone. Follow similar procedures whenever possible for playing legato octaves on the black keys.

In passages which combine black and white keys, play the thumb near the black keys to avoid the wasted motion of moving the hand in and out of the black keys. Also, slide from a black key to a white to help the legato. (The fifth finger can also do this.) The reverse situation, from white key to black, is harder to do, since the distance from the bottom of a depressed white key to the top of an undepressed black one is greater. With practice, however, the resulting break can be made relatively unobtrusive.   61

Double sixths

Vengerova's fingering for major scales in double sixths (playing two notes a sixth apart for each hand) shows only where the third finger would be played, since that finger is used only once in an octave and the other fingerings can be derived from it. This can be seen in the following model:

R.H.

Model fingering for a scale played in sixths by one hand.

Fingerings for major scales in double sixths. (The tonic is the upper note at the start.) The third finger is on:

Scale	L.H.	R.H.	Scale	L.H.	R.H.	Scale	L.H.	R.H.	Scale	L.H.	R.H.
G	g	e	E	g#	c#	D^b	a^b	a^b	B^b	f	a
D	g	b	B	g#	g#	A^b	e^b	a^b	F	c	a
A	g#	f#	F#	g#	d#	E^b	b^b	a^b			

C major is an exception. Madame preferred to alternate either $\frac{5\text{-}4}{1\text{-}2}$ or $\frac{4\text{-}5}{1\text{-}2}$ in both hands, and not to use the third finger at all. $\quad \frac{4\text{-}5}{2\text{-}1}$

It was emphasized that these scales should be learned well hands separately before putting them together. It was understood that they would be practiced with as legato a touch as possible.

C. Leaps

Vengerova taught me three basic principles for learning and playing leaps:

(1) Practice them without looking, either with the eyes closed or with the head turned away. By doing this you learn to gauge the distance better utilizing your other senses. Vengerova was wise enough, however, not to ask me to do this in performance, for it is safer to have all resources available then. Indeed, for the opening of the Chopin Etude, Op. 25, No. 8 (Example 6-3), she suggested that I learn the right hand extra well so that it would not need much attention when playing, thus permitting me to concentrate on the tricky leaps in the left hand.

Example 6-3. Chopin, Etude Op. 25, No. 8 in D^b Major (Leipzig: Breitkopf und Härtel, 1833), measure 1.

(2) When leaping to the fifth finger, open the hand so that the fifth finger is at an angle to the keys. This reduces the distance the arm must travel by increasing the stretch three or more inches. (Vengerova taught me this principle very early in the course of my study.) The left-hand part of the Chopin etude just discussed (Example 6-3) would be played this way. (See photo 14, p. 20.)

(3) Prepare leaps whenever possible by placing the fingers in contact with the keys for at least an instant before playing. This gives greater control and security. Vengerova's directions to Lilian Kallir for practicing the notoriously treacherous coda of the second movement of the Schumann Fantasy (Example 6-4) will illustrate this, among other points.

Example 6-4. Schumann, Fantasy in C Major, Op. 17, second movement, measures 232-33.

There is no time to prepare the leaps occurring on the beats, but one can prepare the leaps to the sixteenth notes by getting there as soon as possible. In addition to insuring that they will be played more accurately, this provides a brief, but much needed, point of repose during each beat. In general, Vengerova said that most people concentrate too much on the leaps which occur on each beat and give insufficient attention to the sixteenth-note chords. To help learn them more firmly, they should be practiced with reverse accents—accenting each sixteenth note and not the eighth note.

Incidentally, Lilian Kallir played the passage as written, and did not rearrange it, as is often done, by putting three notes in the left hand and one in the right.

D. Trills

Vengerova assigned many trill exercises, particularly those which involved holding one or more fingers down while a pair of fingers trilled. The first six of the Pischna exercises fell into this last category, as did some of the Tausig. When discussing the Tausig exercise No. 18, she suggested modifying it, as shown, to convert it into a trill exercise (Example 6-5).

Example 6-5. Tausig-Ehrlich, *Daily Studies for the Piano,* Study 18, written for one hand only. (a) Measure 1. (b) Vengerova's modification of it.

Although Vengerova never discussed their benefits, it would appear that trill exercises are useful not only to prepare for playing trills, but to strengthen the fingers for many types of figuration.

Other than assigning exercises, Vengerova had relatively little to say about developing a good trill technique. Once she recommended playing trills with the second and fourth fingers since they were about equal in length, and thus made a good pair. Vengerova apparently approached this subject in the same way as she did other aspects of technique, a point which was confirmed by Jacob Lateiner and Barbara Elliott Bailey. When I asked her how to practice trills, she told me only to use her system of accents beginning with "ones," and proceeding through "twos," "threes," "fours," etc.

Chapter VII

Staccato, and Staccato Octaves

A. Staccato

Staccato playing should be combined with the up and down wrist motions so characteristic of the Vengerova technique, so that one drops on accents and raises between them. This avoids stiffness and makes it easier to phrase and add shadings to the music.

Vengerova played staccato using both non-percussive and percussive touches. A non-percussive touch is one in which the finger is in contact with the keys before playing. A percussive touch is one in which the fingertip hits the key from above. This distinction will be observed when classifying the different touches used.

(1) Non-percussive touches (most often required of me):

(a) Depress the key with the finger; then lift it quickly from the key.

(b) Pluck the key with the finger as if snapping a rubber band. (This is often needed to achieve the desired crispness.) To accomplish this, pull the fingertip sharply inward toward the palm of the hand at the very moment when the key is being depressed. This keeps the fingertip in contact with the key only briefly and produces a very short note. This touch is effective in this excerpt from the last movement of the Beethoven Sonata in E^b, Op. 7 (Example 7-1), particularly in the softer bars where it gives the needed crispness without being too loud.

Example 7-1. Beethoven, Sonata in E^b Major, Op. 7, fourth movement, measures 124-26.

(It should be noted that I do not remember ever having the

distinction between categories (a) and (b) pointed out to me, but am aware of it from observing my own playing.)

(c) When you depress the keys with the fingertips, snap the hand away from the keyboard while bending at the wrist, thus pulling the fingertips from the keys. This is used primarily for chords or intervals, though it can be adapted to single notes if desired. (I used this type of staccato least of all.) The Vengerova wrist accent can be combined with this. Indeed, it would be required in the accompaniment hand of perpetual-motion etudes when practiced in the Vengerova style—see p. 42—like Example 7-2 from Clementi's *Gradus ad Parnassum.*

Example 7-2. Clementi, *Gradus ad Parnassum* (Tausig edition), Etude No. 1, measures 1-3.

(2) Percussive touch. Move the hand as a unit from the wrist and direct a relatively fixed and firm finger onto the key. (This is the only percussive touch Vengerova ever taught regularly for use in performance.) Although it is not in contact with the key beforehand, the fingertip should be close to it to prevent loss of speed and accuracy. (My own observations suggest that to avoid tension the wrist should not be low.) Vengerova suggested practicing scales in single notes this way to develop facility in this technique.

This touch can be reproduced away from the piano by bouncing the hand rapidly on a desk while maintaining a quiet and level forearm. Note that the power comes on the down movement of the hand as it directs the fingertip into the key.

This touch is particularly useful for fast passages with many staccato notes in a row, where it might be difficult to prepare and pluck each finger from the key in the time allotted. This also permits one to achieve an evenness of sound more readily because the hand is transmitting the same amount of weight into each fingertip. In the last movement of the Schumann Concerto (Example 7-3), Vengerova suggested using this touch, despite the portamento markings, to give the proper crispness.

66

Example 7-3. Schumann, Concerto in A Minor, Op. 54, third movement, measures 105-09.

It is possible to combine touches (1b) and (2) so that the hand is bounced from the wrist and the finger is plucked slightly when the key is hit. I never discussed this with Vengerova, but it probably would not have mattered to her as long as one added the usual Vengerova wrist motion to the combination, and the resultant sound was good. The importance of the last cannot be exaggerated. Chords must be carefully balanced for all staccato touches, and a percussive staccato must never become noisy and hard.

These are the chief staccato touches that Vengerova taught me. At no time did she illustrate a touch in which the fingers are thrown percussively on the keys while the wrist remans quiet. But I never played for her a passage requiring a very fast perpetual-motion staccato like that of the right hand of the third etude in Schumann's *Symphonic Etudes,* which goes faster than the excerpt from his Concerto. Hence I cannot say how she would have handled that type of problem.

Here are two illustrations of staccato combined with other touches:

(1) When one plays a two-note slur accenting the first note, one drops the wrist on the first note and lifts it on the second. Lifting the wrist on the second note helps one to play softer, since less weight is directed into the keys. This motion is usually made in a leisurely manner, but the second note can be played staccato with an abrupt upward motion of the wrist which pulls the finger off the key. The same approach can be used for three or more connected notes which begin with an accent and end with a staccato.

(2) At the start of the development section of the first movement of the Schumann G Minor Sonata (Example 7-4), a melodic line, marked staccato, alternates with a repeated note in the same hand which must be played quietly. Vengerova said to throw the hand on the staccato notes. When played this way the hand is rocked (rotated) back and forth with the weight going into the fingers which play staccato. Since their

motions are begun slightly above the key, they are played percussively. However, all movements must be fairly small since this is a soft passage, and too much weight should not be directed into the keys.

Example 7-4. Schumann, Sonata in G Minor, Op. 22, first movement, measures 93-96.

The staccato dots probably indicate accents as much as staccato, a fact that may have influenced Vengerova's directions to me.

B. Staccato Octaves

While Vengerova made many valuable comments throughout the years on how to play staccato octaves, she did not have as rigorous a method of teaching them as she did for most other aspects of piano playing. Olga Stroumillo, her assistant and close friend, even stated categorically that Vengerova did not have any system at all of teaching staccato octaves. Jacob Lateiner and Barbara Elliott Bailey put it differently. Both said that Vengerova approached the study of octaves in the same way as she did other facets of piano playing.

Many slower passages can be played comfortably using a non-percussive touch and the usual Vengerova technique. But when one plays faster the essential problem of staccato octave playing becomes apparent: how to achieve speed and power without stiffening up, even though the same fingers and muscles must be used again and again. One solution is to play octaves with a bounce of the hand from the wrist, allowing the fingertips to hit the keys percussively. This motion is similar to staccato touch (2), as described on p. 66, and is a standard octave technique used by many teachers. Certainly the instructions found in the introduction to C. H. Döring's *Exercises and Studies on the Pianoforte for the Preparation and Development of Staccato Octave Playing,*[21] which Vengerova assigned to me, advocated this approach.

[21]New York: G. Schirmer, 1902.

Initially, however, I confused these directions with the usual Vengerova rise and fall of the wrist and did not realize then that something new was indicated. Later I understood the difference, but unfortunately did not discuss it with Vengerova, and so I cannot present her exact thoughts on the matter.

The two types of motion are basically very different. The staccato octave touch requires that the forearm be kept level while the hand and fingertips are bounced percussively on the keys. In the usual Vengerova wrist motion the fingertips are kept close to the keys while the forearm is moved up and down pivoting at the wrist. The elbow is kept quiet in both cases.

It is possible, of course, to combine the two motions, and that is what a Vengerova pupil would do to help play octaves musically. In this case the wrist and forearm are raised and lowered, the hand and fingertips are bounced on the keys, and the elbow is kept quiet. This is the way I consciously played staccato octaves during much of my study with Vengerova.

It must be stated, though, that when I played loudly, I probably brought other muscles and techniques into use, without quite knowing then what I was doing, because it is difficult for me to play staccato octaves *forte* while using only the wrist to achieve power.

The practice technique of this Döring exercise (Example 7-5) was particularly recommended for developing the flexibility of the wrist in octave playing.

Example 7-5. Döring, *Exercises and Studies on the Pianoforte for the Preparation and Development of Staccato Octave Playing* (G. Shirmer, 1902), p. 4, measures 1-8. The left hand plays the same exercise two octaves lower.

Döring's collection also contains helpful etudes and a variety of exercises, including some to develop facility in playing leaps and interlocking patterns.

Here are some additional suggestions for octave playing made to me by Vengerova and, in one case, her assistant Mildred Jones. The first three are general principles that must be applied where appropriate; the next two are procedures that may be used for practicing.

(1) When playing an octave on the white keys which precedes or follows one on the black keys, play the thumb and fifth fingers close to the black keys. This avoids the wasted motion and lost speed caused by moving in and out of the black keys.

(2) Lead with the thumb, rather than the fifth or fourth fingers in playing octaves. This gives greater control.

(3) Adjust the level of the fingers and hand to the differing heights of black and white keys. (This was told to me by Mildred Jones.)

(4) Practice each voice of the octave separately. It is particularly helpful to do this with the thumb.

(5) Practice a passage by repeating the notes several times in a row as in Exercise 7a.

Exercise 7a.

Vengerova suggested that the difficult right-hand passage from Schumann's Novellette in E Major (Example 7-6) be practiced according to the procedures given below:

Example 7-6. Schumann, Novellette in E Major, Op. 21, No. 7, measures 13-16.

(a) Experiment with the fingering. Choose anything that will work.

(b) Learn to play the leaps "blindfolded," i.e., either by looking away from the keyboard or with the eyes closed.

(c) Make an exercise out of the passage like Exercise 7b.

70

Exercise 7b.

It is a matter of controversy whether to use the fourth or fifth finger on the black keys when playing octaves. The fourth seems more convenient, but some pianists and pedagogues claim that it sounds weaker than the fifth. Vengerova never discussed the issue except for indicating that she preferred the fifth when leaping to an octave on the black keys. Apparently my choice of the fourth finger was otherwise acceptable.

At no time did Vengerova suggest any special hand position to be used when playing octaves.[22]

Exercise 7c (which Vengerova gave to me during my first year of study with her) helps develop the flexibility of the thumb when playing staccato, and thus provides good preparation for staccato octave playing.

Exercise 7c. (*The quarter notes are all played by the thumb.*)

The thumb is thrown percussively on the key, with the curvature of its first joint increasing as it approaches the fifth finger. This exercise is first played slowly and then gradually faster. Initially the thumb is held fairly high above the key before playing, but as the tempo increases it

[22]As an example of what is meant, let me quote from József Gát, *The Technique of Piano Playing,* 2nd ed. (London: Collet's Holdings Ltd., 1965), p. 147, footnote 2: "When playing octaves some players will slightly bend their second and possibly even their third fingers in order to increase the firmness of the whole hand." Gát then discusses the merits and demerits of doing this.

gradually moves closer.

This exercise also helps the thumb first joint acquire the curvature needed for playing scales in single notes. Indeed, Vengerova may have given it to me for that purpose. (Photo 15 on p. 20 shows the proper curvature of the right hand thumb when playing G in bar two of the exercise.) The strength and flexibility of the rotary muscles of the arm also profit, because the hand pivots on the fixed fifth finger while all of the motion takes place on the thumb side.

Chapter VIII

Fingering

Vengerova's approach to fingering was highly flexible. She would generally ignore the topic if all went well, but if it had not, she would often suggest a different fingering, even one that went against her usual procedures. (I dreaded having a lesson if I had not practiced a passage sufficiently, because she would then change its fingering.)

Her first choices tended to be straightforward and uncomplicated, as is suggested by rules (2), (3), and (6) given below. This was practical because her students did not rely only on finger articulation, which more elaborate fingerings tend to emphasize, but could achieve many affects by proper relaxation, adjustments of hand position and the wrist, and differing applications of weight.

These same procedures helped her pupils' legato, as did the ease with which her students transferred the weight from one tone to the next. But she also insisted that the best fingering for legato be chosen whenever that touch was needed, and that a good legato be achieved if possible without the assistance of the pedal.

Vengerova seems to have had these basic principles for choosing specific fingering:

(1) Let the musical effect take priority over pianistic convenience when the two conflict. (An awkward fingering is preferable to an easier one if it leads to a superior result musically.)

(2) Use the whole hand (all five fingers) whenever possible to cut down on the number of changes of hand position. (This helps to attain speed and ease of performance, and makes the fingering less fussy.)

(3) Use the same finger on repeated notes unless, of course, the passage is so fast or the repetition goes on for so long that this becomes impractical or impossible. (Changing fingers is often harder physically and requires greater concentration.)

(4) Divide a passage between the hands if it is more comfortable that way and does not inhibit the musical result.

(5) Use the thumb, which is a strong finger, when a heavy accent is required, even on the black keys. Use weaker fingers (second and fourth) to avoid accents in quiet lyrical moments.

(6) Follow a regular scale and arpeggio fingering, if possible, when such passages occur in the literature. (While this point may seem

obvious to some, if only because it is easier to use a fingering which has already been learned, not all teachers advocate this approach.)

(7) Use the fifth finger on the outside of a chord whenever possible to get better balance.

(8) Do the following to help play legato:

   (a) Substitute one finger silently for another.

   (b) Slide from black key to white.

   (c) Cross longer fingers over the shorter ones (e.g., 4 over 5).

   (d) Pass shorter fingers under longer ones (e.g., 5 under 4).

(Some of these procedures may seem awkward initially, but with time they become perfectly natural and enhance the musical effect.)

Here are some examples of these procedures. All fingerings are Vengerova's except where indicated.

This passage from a Mendelssohn etude (Example 8-1) represents one of the few times that Vengerova gave me a specific fingering (the bottom one) for a passage before I played the piece. She chose to have the whole hand cover as many notes as possible, thus avoiding finger crossings (Rule 2) and making it easier to achieve the needed speed.

Example 8-1. Mendelssohn, Etude in F, Op. 104, No. 2, measures 85-87 (beginning). Copyright, 1928, by G. Schirmer, Inc. Reproduced by permission. *The top fingering is by the editor, Edwin Hughes; the bottom fingering is Vengerova's.*

In this passage from the Schumann Concerto (Example 8-2) Vengerova again preferred to use the whole hand in an extended position (Rule 2) for the opening left hand arpeggios rather than to cross over. This procedure also permits the left hand thumb (a strong finger) to play the accented A^b in bar 69 (Rule 5). The division of hands in bar 70 (Rule 4) requires that the pedal hold down the *sforzando* chord in the right hand.

Example 8-2. Schumann, Piano Concerto in A Minor, Op. 54, first movement, measures 67-71 (beginning).

The Schubert (Example (8-3) and Kabalevsky (Example 8-4) pieces both reveal her preference for using the same finger on repeated notes (Rule 3). The Schubert also shows how she recommended using all five fingers on the upbeat to avoid extra crossings (Rule 2) as well as the thumb on the strong beat (Rule 5).

Example 8-3. Schubert, Sonata in A major, Op. 120 (D.V. 644), third movement, measures 1-4 (beginning).

Example 8-4. Kabalevsky, Sonata No. 3, Op. 46, third movement, measures 1-4. Copyright (c) 1950 by INTERNATIONAL MUSIC CO. Copyright renewed. All rights reserved. Used by permission of INTERNATIONAL MUSIC CO.

Examples 8-5 to 8-7 reveal how she often divided a passage between two hands to relieve the strain on one hand (Rule 4). (It makes me sad to see an unfortunate student struggle through Chopin's "Revolutionary" Etude without this help.) The Moszkowski passages also illustrate how careful planning and use of the whole hand (Rule 2) reduce the number of crossings, which tend to slow one down, to a minimum.

Example 8-5. Chopin, Etude Op. 10, No. 12, "Revolutionary" (Leipzig: Kistner, 1833), measure 9.

Example 8-6. Weber, *Perpetual Motion* (fourth movement from the Sonata in C Major, Op. 24), measures 292-95 (beginning).

(a)

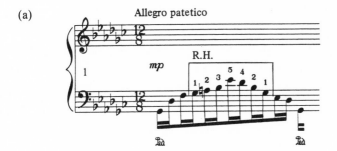

(b)

Example 8-7. Moszkowski, Etude in G^b Major, Op. 24, No. 1 (a) Beginning of measure 1. (b) Measure 45. Copyright, 1915, by G. Schirmer, Inc. Edited by August Fraemcke. Reproduced by permission.

Examples 8-8 and 8-9 illustrate the use of the thumb on a strong beat to achieve an accent regardless of the apparent inconvenience (Rules 1 and 5). The Schumann (8-8) provides a particularly striking illustration of this approach, because the desired effect, both musically and technically, is easily achieved with this fingering. In the Chopin (8-9) bars 603 and 629 also illustrate this. Example 8-9b also shows an effective division of a passage between the hands (Rule 4) with a minimum number of crossings and the use of the whole hand (Rule 2). Note at the end of the example that the low bass note is played with two fingers of the left hand for additional strength.

Example 8-8. Schumann, Piano Concerto in A Minor, Op. 54, third movement, measures 57-65 (beginning).

Example 8-9. Chopin, Scherzo in C# Minor, Op. 39 (Leipzig: Breitkopf und Härtel, 1840). (a) Measures 601-04. (b) Measures 627-33.

Example 8-10 shows how an awkward leap can be avoided in the left hand by sliding the thumb from black key to white (Rule 8b).

Example 8-10. Chopin, Scherzo in C# Minor, Op. 39 (Leipzig: Breitkopf und Härtel, 1840), measures 257-58.

Examples 8-11 and 8-12 illustrate how Vengerova often made ingenious use of the technique of crossing the longer fingers over the shorter (Rule 8c). (This is essential for much legato playing, particularly in double notes, but is often neglected elsewhere.) In both excerpts the third finger crosses over the fifth. In the Moszkowski (8-12) Vengerova's fingering for the left hand is preferable to the editor's to produce the big accent she wanted (and wrote in my score) on the C-natural in the bass.

Example 8-11. Beethoven, Piano Concerto No. 1 in C Major, Op. 15, third movement, measures 15-17 (beginning).

Example 8-12. Moszkowski, Etude in G^b Major, Op. 24, No. 1, measures 17-18 (beginning). Copyright, 1915, by G. Schirmer, Inc. Reproduced by permission. *The upper fingering is by the editor, August Graemcke; the lower fingering is Vengerova's. The pedaling, which I used, is the editor's.*

The next two examples illustrate fingerings which do not follow neatly any of the above rules.

Near the conclusion of this passage from the Schumann Concerto (Example 8-13), the right hand can best match the sound of the left hand octaves by using only the third finger.

Example 8-13. Schumann, Piano Concerto in A Minor, Op. 54, first movement, measures 45-47.

Vengerova found an unusual fingering to help when my right hand tired excessively in this passage by Beethoven (Example 8-14). (I was only fifteen and had just become her pupil.) Instead of playing it with only the second finger on each D as I had been doing, Vengerova suggested inserting the thumb on some of them to relieve the strain of the tremolo position. I have added some fingerings (in parentheses) to those found in my edition to make clear how this section was to be performed.

80

Example 8-14. Beethoven, Sonata in E^b Major, Op. 7, first movement, measures 111-13.

Vengerova's fingering for the chromatic scale has a somewhat unusual feature when the right hand ascends and the left hand descends: the alternation of 1 and 2 whenever possible instead of the more usual 1 and 3. It is possible that Vengerova learned this from Leschetizky, for this fingering is found in *The Groundwork of the Leschetizky Method, Issued with His Approval by His Assistant Malwine Brée.*[23]

Vengerova's fingering for the chromatic scale.

[23]New York: G. Schirmer, 1902, p. 21.

Chapter IX

EXCEPTIONS TO THE STANDARD VENGEROVA TECHNIQUE

The first five examples given below illustrate how Vengerova could modify her usual approach to technique when it was not helping the student. She made these comments to help my playing at particular lessons and possibly might not have done so if my performances had sounded differently.

(1) Percussive singing tone

Vengerova remarked that I would get a better sound on the opening chord of the first theme of the Schumann Concerto (Example 9-1) if I approached it from above, that is percussively, rather than having my finger in contact with the key beforehand. On one or two other occasions she may have made the same suggestion, which was unusual for her, but this is the only example I can clearly recall. Probably I was not getting sufficient weight into the keyboard for a good singing tone, and so Vengerova waived her rule against playing with a percussive touch in the hope that it would help achieve the desired effect.

Example 9-1. Schumann, Piano Concerto in A Minor, Op. 54, first movement, measures 12-13.

(2) Lengthening Notes

In a passage from the Chopin C# Minor Scherzo (Example 9-2), Vengerova suggested that I hold the right hand thumb briefly beyond its marked duration on the third eighth-note of each bar. This made it easier to play the top notes by giving some support to the hand. Although contrary to the normal practice of lifting one's fingers after the duration marked for the notes, it made the passage easier for me. It is unlikely that listeners would hear what I was doing, but if they did, the results would be acceptable, because the pitches being prolonged had already been emphasized.

Example 9-2. Chopin, Scherzo in C♯ Minor, Op. 39 (Leipzig: Breitkopf und Härtel, 1840), measures 585-88. The original is without fingering.

(3) Passagework with flat hands

In another part of the same Chopin scherzo (Example 9-3) it was difficult for me to play softly enough in the pasagework which begins in measure 159. To produce the needed translucent sound Vengerova suggested that I play with flat hands and little arch and with a flat fifth finger on my right hand (see photo 16, p. 20), thus making it easier to play softly. (She usually required a cupped and arched hand position with a somewhat curved fifth finger.)

Example 9-3. Chopin, Scherzo in C♯ Minor, Op. 39 (Leipzig: Breitkopf und Härtel, 1840), measures 152-163. The original is without fingering.

In addition to this exception to her technique she had some other interesting points to make about this passage:

(a) The left hand should be higher than the right, and held towards the back of the keyboard to avoid collisions with the right.

(b) In bar 161 a slight accent should be made on the D^bs on the downbeat to help give rhythmic coherence to the passage. Her fingering helped to achieve this, not only by using the strong left hand thumb, but by requiring that the positions of the fingers in both hands be shifted slightly at that point, which automatically tends to produce an accent.

(c) The left hand wrist should be tilted slightly to the left using the rotary muscles. This is more comfortable, and also makes it easier to get the thumb under the hand.

(4) Not transferring arm weight

In this excerpt from Liszt's *Waldesrauschen* (Example 9-4), Vengerova wanted me to avoid playing accents on the grace notes by putting a little extra pressure on the preceding notes after sounding them. The arm weight should not be transferred from one fingertip to the next as usual, and the grace notes should be played only with fingertip pressure.

Example 9-4. Liszt, *Waldesrauschen,* measure 7.

(5) Use of stiff wrist

In this passage from Liszt's *Un Sospiro* (Example 9-5) Vengerova suggested that I play the accented left hand chords with a stiff wrist to get more power, instead of having the wrist fall as usual. (Apparently the chords had been too weak.) In between each chord I relaxed, of course.

Example 9-5. Liszt, *Un Sospiro,* measures 34-35.

(6) Accents with shallow drops

When I was playing this chromatic scale from the same work (Example 9-6) Vengerova suggested that fast passages like this one should be practiced in "twos" and "threes" without too much motion. This practice technique is also closer to the way the scale would actually be performed, since the scale can't be played fast with much motion. Practice time could then be saved since accents made with shallow drops can be played more quickly than those with the customary deeper drops. Obviously Vengerova would not have suggested this to somebody who was not already well grounded in her technique. (This excerpt also appears on p. 96 of the chapter on pedaling as part of Example 10-12.)

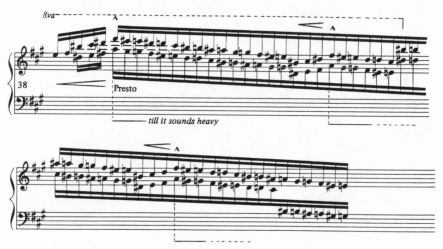

Example 9-6. Liszt, *Un Sospiro,* measure 38.

(7) High Finger Accent

Florence Frantz Vennett Snyder told me that when she first became Vengerova's assistant in the early 1930s, Vengerova suggested to her that a high finger accent could be used as an exercise to strengthen fingers. A very firm finger would be made to strike the key from a high point and then to relax immediately afterward. This practice technique, to be done only slowly, could be used to help weak fingers or caved-in knuckles. Vengerova recommended using this exercise only as a means to overcome a specific problem when practicing and, in keeping with her customary opposition to the use of high fingers, did not advocate playing this way.

Chapter X

Pedaling

Pedaling was important to Vengerova, and she devoted much time to it at lessons. While she never gave a formal lecture on the topic, she did express to me the various principles on which her pedaling was based. I have collected and numbered them and have selected some examples as illustration.

All rules refer to the damper pedal, since it was in its use that Vengerova made her chief contribution. Lifting the dampers off the strings affects the piano sonority by ensuring (1) that a note will continue to sound until the strings stop vibrating of their own accord, and (2) that the tone quality of each note will be enriched by sympathetic vibration from the other strings which vibrate for their entire length or in partials (overtones). This last feature gives greater warmth and resonance to the piano tone.

Unfortunately, while the pedal may enrich the piano tone, thus avoiding a dry sonority, its use may also bring about blurred harmonies and a loss of clarity, since all notes will continue to sound. Often these problems arise, regardless of the sonority desired, because of the need to sustain important notes. A composer for the orchestra could solve these difficulties by giving one group of instruments the harmonies and another the melody. Solo pianists, however, do not have such resources available to them. Vengerova's solutions to the problems presented by such situations are always interesting and frequently ingenious.

Two other factors must be considered now. First, blurring caused by the pedal is more likely to be acceptable in a faster tempo, when it will not last as long, than in a slower one. Second, it is also possible to depress the pedal only part way, so that the dampers permit the strings to vibrate only partially ("half damping"), or to change the pedal without letting the dampers fall completely, so that the change is not a clean one ("half pedaling"). There is some confusion about these terms, however, and many people use "half pedaling" for both cases, as I will in future paragraphs. Each of these types of pedaling is a compromise, since the pedal is used or changed only partially, so that some, but not all, of the sonority is kept. Both make possible many subtle effects which could not otherwise be achieved.

According to Lilian Kallir, Vengerova often discussed half pedaling and made it an important and valuable part of her teaching. My own experience was different, for she seldom mentioned it to me (which shows how her teaching could vary from student to student). I have included among the examples, however, one of the few passages for which she suggested half pedaling.

While Vengerova's principles of pedaling will be stated as rules, they are not absolutes and cannot be applied mechanically. There are too many variables in pedaling, pianism in general, and music to permit that to happen. She herself made this clear by emphasizing that one must adjust the pedaling to the touch of the pianist, the piano itself, and to the acoustics of the room. For example, a person playing in a dry room or on a rather dead piano might need more pedal than otherwise. Furthermore, a person with a shallow tone might need more pedal than one with a richer sound. Her instructions on pedaling a specific passage, therefore, were tailored to the needs of a particular student. In addition, differing conceptions of a passage might also require varied kinds of pedaling. Nevertheless, these principles and the accompanying illustrations should be of interest and value to most pianists.

Vengerova's rules of pedaling:

(1) Time the pedaling by one of these ways:

(a) *Syncopated (legato) pedaling.* Hold the old chord on the pedal until the new chord is played. Release the pedal at that moment and depress it again immediately. (Among other things this method permits playing chords legato by means of the pedal when the fingers alone cannot accomplish this.)

(b) *Non-legato pedaling.* Release the pedal on the previous chord before playing the new chord in the following situations:

1. A non-legato sound is desired.

2. The previous chord would otherwise get too heavy.

3. A melodic outline must stand out clearly when the old chord is dying away.

4. Too much blurring would otherwise result—e.g., after a modulation a new chord needs to be caught quickly with a very clean pedal.

(2) Pedal according to the harmonies. Harmonic requirements take precedence over melodic ones.

(3) Catch the bass of the harmony on the pedal, particularly when it can't be held by a finger.

(4) Change the pedal when the bass changes, even if the shift is only from root position to first inversion of the same chord.

(5) Pedal more lightly in the bass register than the treble, because the ear tolerates less blurring there. This is particularly true for the intervals of seconds heard melodically.

(6) Pedal descending melodic lines with discretion. More blurring is tolerable on ascending ones. (If a descending line is pedaled, the previously played tones will make it harder for the new tones to project, since a higher-pitched note tends to cover a lower one.)

(7) Reinforce an accent with the pedal.

(8) Plan pedaling to avoid unwanted accents. Both depressing and lifting the pedal abruptly create accents. (Depressing the pedal increases the resonance by sympathetic vibration; lifting it produces a negative accent, because the sudden absence of sound stands out.)

(9) Adjust pedaling to the dynamics involved. More pedal is acceptable in *forte* than in *piano.*

(10 Don't pedal through rests, or notes which are staccato or non-legato.

(11) Use less pedal on the weaker beats of the bar when they should sound lighter, particularly the last one.

(12) Adjust pedaling to the phrasing.

(13) Lift the pedal on the second and weaker note of a two-note slur, even if the chord remains the same (e.g., ♩ ♪♩ ♪).

(14) Avoid pedaling each chord in a fast tempo with rapid harmonic movement, since it is hard to avoid some blurring under those circumstances. In such a case it might be better to do without pedal entirely.

(15) Match the pedaling to the style of the composition. A degree of pedaling that would be appropriate for Chopin would be out of place in Mozart.

(16) Adjust the pedaling to the touch of the pianist, the nature of the piano, and the acoustics of the room. (See p. 88 for details.)

(17) Depress the pedal only part way, if desired, so that a portion of the sound is kept, or else change it only partially so that some of the old sound still remains (half pedaling). (See pp. 87-88 for details.)

In the following illustrations of these rules I have given Vengerova's pedaling and, in those cases where he also marked it, the composer's. Most examples present situations in which at least two rules conflict with each other in order to show how Vengerova resolved such problems. The tables on pp. 97 and 98 show in which of these examples she followed (or broke) these rules.

The dramatic opening of this stormy and highly accented Scherzo (Example 10-1) demands playing with a big sonority. Yet if one respects Schumann's rests, the effect is vitiated. Vengerova ignored them and pedaled through the entire bar, thus sustaining the bass and helping to create a striking beginning. (Schumann merely wrote "Pedal" in this example and the next without indicating where it should be applied.)

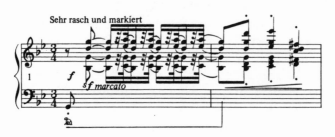

Example 10-1. Schumann, Sonata in G Minor, Op. 22, third movement: Scherzo, measures 1-2.

In this *Novellette* (Example 10-2) the need to support with pedal the bass line and harmonies in bars 2-5, the *crescendo* in bar 3, and the *sforzando* in bar 5 clashes with the staccato articulation found in each bar. The staccati are destroyed by Vengerova's pedaling, but only for brief moments at a time, so that the playful quality of the theme is maintained.

Example 10-2. Schumann, *Novellette* in E Major, Op. 21, No. 7, measures 1-6.

A change of pedaling can add color to a repetition of a theme. For this Kabalevsky phrase (Example 10-3) Vengerova suggested omitting pedal at its first entrance at the end of bar 28, which also makes playing *pianissimo* easier, and using pedal later at the end of bar 34 for contrast when the pitch is higher and the dynamic marking louder.

90

Example 10-3. Kabalevsky, Sonata No. 3, Op. 46, third movement. Copyright ©
1950 by INTERNATIONAL MUSIC CO. Copyright renewed. All rights reserved.
Used by permission of INTERNATIONAL MUSIC CO. (a) Measures 28-30.
(b) Measures 34-36.

Poulenc often said that his piano music needed lots of pedal to
capture the right style. In Example 10-4 Vengerova's pedaling softens
the outlines of theme to give the needed color and charm. Depressing
the pedal only partly (half pedaling) and removing it on the weak beats
keep the blurring tasteful. Originally Vengerova wanted each pedal held
for an additional sixteenth-note, but she later changed her mind.

Example 10-4. Poulenc, Suite for Piano, second movement (London: J. & W.
Chester, Ltd., 1926), measure 1. Quoted by permission.

The mood is fiery in both excerpts from Mendelssohn's *Scherzo a
Capriccio* (Example 10-5), and the need to reinforce the *sforzandi*
with the pedal is obvious. Although this briefly breaches other rules by
pedaling through a non-legato descending line in bar 13 and a short rest
in bar 22, the fast tempo helps make this perfectly acceptable.

Example 10-5. Mendelssohn, *Scherzo a Cappriccio.* (a) Measures 13-14. (b) Measures 21-22.

Because this climactic passage (Example 10-6) requires a rich sonority and support for the arpeggiated harmonies, pedal is required even though the melodic line descends. Fortunately, the relatively high register and fast tempo make this acceptable, particularly when the left hand is not too heavy. Observe that the pedal changes to show the shift from root position to first inversion.

Example 10-6. Mendelssohn, Fantasy in F# Minor, Op. 28, third movement, measures 23-24 (beginning).

Vengerova found one of her most subtle pedalings for Chopin's *Fantasie-Impromptu* (Example 10-7). Bar 5 of it bears some resemblance to the Mendelssohn excerpt just discussed—the accompaniments are identical although a fifth apart—and one might be tempted to pedal them the same way. But putting a new pedal down on the second half of the bar creates an accent, which Vengerova felt reduced its elegance. To avoid this she wanted the pedal removed (thus also eliminating some of the blurring), but not on the D# in the middle of the bar where expected. Instead, it was to be lifted on the next note to avoid calling attention to the D# by a sudden cessation of sound—a negative accent. (Chopin's own pedaling is unworkable on modern pianos unless modified by half pedaling.)

Example 10-7. Chopin, *Fantaisie-Impromptu,* Op. 66 (Berlin: A.M. Schlesinger, 1855), measures 1-6.

Because of the striking modulation in Example 10-8, Vengerova felt that a very clean pedal was needed at the start of bar 55 to clarify the change in harmony. Since the pedal must be caught quickly to hold the bass, she suggested releasing the previous pedal a little early to avoid any blurring. In bar 55 she said to take off the pedal on the fifth or sixth note of each group depending on the piano.

Chopin's own pedaling is probably a legato one. In his time it was customary to put an asterisk before a new pedal sign, regardless of whether a break in continuity of sonority was desired. (Example 5-1 on p. 46 shows this clearly.)

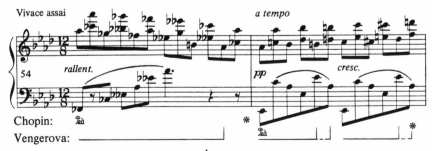

Example 10-8. Chopin, Etude in A^b Major, Op. 10, No. 10 (Leipzig: Kistner, 1833), measures 54-55.

The pianist must project the contrasting characters of the repeated notes and legato bars in Example 10-9. The sound would be too dry if pedal were completely eliminated, so Vengerova suggested keeping it down for one beat in the staccato bars and for two in the legato. It was completely removed on the third beat to lighten the sonority and give the typical dance character of a fast waltz.

Chopin's own pedaling is still workable on today's pianos, although heavier in sound. Vengerova may not have been familiar with it, since the original editions of his music were no longer readily available in her day, and accurate reprints (Paderewski, Henle, and Vienna Urtext editions) had not yet appeared.

Example 10-9. Chopin, Waltz No. 1 in E^b, Op. 18 (Leipzig: Breitkopf und Härtel, 1834), measures 21-24.

The need for resonance at a climax of this mazurka (Example 10-10) justifies pedaling through descending seconds and short rests. The pedal is released, however, on the last beat of the bar to avoid too thick a sonority.

Example 10-10. Chopin, C# Minor Mazurka, Op. 41, No. 1 (Leipzig: Breitkopf und Härtel, 1840), measures 119-21.

Staccato marks frequently seem to imply a crisp attack on a note rather than releasing it quickly, particularly in Romantic music. Vengerova apparently interpreted the opening of the Paganini-Liszt Etude No. 6 (Example 10-11) that way, for she wanted it pedaled throughout the entire first beat despite the rests. This avoids dryness and is closer to the sound of Paganini's original, which omitted the initial staccato marks. Violin tone also resonates longer after the release of a note than does piano tone, which suggests a less-than-literal treatment of rests if one wishes to imitate violin sound on the piano.

Example 10-11. Paganini-Liszt, Etude No. 6, measures 1-2.

Liszt's cadenzas, like that in bar 38 of *Un Sospiro* (Example 10-12), require pedal to avoid dryness and to give the needed brilliance and glitter. This blurs the descending chromatic scale, but the style allows it partly because of the high register and fast tempo. Although it is not so marked in my copy, I undoubtedly pedaled each chord in bar 37. To avoid a thick sonority the pedal is changed at the first high F# in bar 38, thus reinforcing that note's accent. It is released when the sound becomes heavy, depressed again at the next accented F#, and so on.

Example 10-12. Liszt, *Un Sospiro,* measures 37-38.

TABLE 1

THE RULES OF PEDALING SIGNIFICANTLY FOLLOWED OR BROKEN BY VENGEROVA IN THE PRECEDING EXAMPLES

Example Number	Rules Followed	Rules Broken	Example Number	Rules Followed	Rules Broken
10-1	1b,3,7,9,10	10	10-7	2,3,8,11,12	4,6
10-2	1b,2,3,7,10,14	7,10	10-8	1b4,2,3,15,16	6
10-3	5,9,10		10-9	1b,2,3,10,11	6,10
10-4	1b,3,6,11,15,17		10-10	1b,7,9,10,11	6,10
10-5	1b,2,3,7,10,11,13	6,10	10-11	1b,2,3,10,11	10
10-6	1a,2,3,4,9	6	10-12	7,9,15,16	6

NOTES: (1) Because rules 10 and 7 may be both followed and broken in different parts of the same example, they may be listed at times in both columns.

(2) Since rules 12, 15, and 16 are almost universally true for good pedaling, the influence of each is recorded for only a limited number of particularly appropriate examples.

(3) Although rule 6 is stated only in a cautionary manner, it appears most informative to list each pedaled descending melodic line as a violation, and to let the reader refer to the description to see what makes it acceptable.

TABLE 2

THE EXAMPLES SIGNIFICANTLY FOLLOWING OR BREAKING EACH RULE OF PEDALING

Rule Number	Followed in Examples	Broken in Examples
1a	6	
1b	1,2,4,5,8,9,10,11	
1b4	8	
2	2,5,6,7,8,9,11	
3	1,2,4,5,6,7,8,9,11	
4	6	7
5	3	
6	4	5,6,7,8,9,10,12
7	1,2,5,10,12	2
8	7	
9	1,3,6,10,12	
10	1,2,3,5,9,10,11	1,2,5,9,10,11
11	4,5,7,9,10,11	
12	7	
13	5	
14	2	
15	4,8,12	
16	8,12	
17	4	

NOTE: The prefix (10-) has been eliminated from the example numbers for simplicity's sake.

Chapter XI

Some Afterthoughts

It now seems appropriate to make a few observations and to raise a few questions which could only be understood properly after completing a description of the Vengerova system.

The first is that her method should be treated as a tool to help one learn and play music, and not as a rigid straitjacket into which all music must be put, whether or not it fits. The motions exist to help produce the desired sound and are not ends in themselves. (Vengerova herself often failed to emphasize this.) When one begins to learn a new piece with a variety of figurations, one need not start by practicing every scale on the first page with accents. Instead one should try to grasp the general shape, feel, and sound of the music in the initial readings, though one should drop with the wrist on melodic accents or solid forte chords even at this stage. Later when one works on the piece in detail one chooses the practice technique needed for a particular passage, including practicing with accents where appropriate. The Vengerova system should be a help in learning a piece quickly and in playing it well. It should not become a series of rituals making it harder rather than easier to learn music.

How effective a teacher would Vengerova be today? Wouldn't it be harder now, almost twenty-five years after her death, for American students, who have been brought up in a tradition which emphasizes their rights and freedoms, to adjust to her methods? A speculative question like this can have no simple answer. The late Irwin Freundlich, the well-known piano pedagogue, told me in 1975 that he doubted whether any major teacher could now require, as Vengerova did, that each pupil play with the same technical system. (She must have had some flexibility in this regard, however, because advanced pianists and artists who were not her regular students came to her for occasional coaching sessions.) But even today's pianists need to follow a disciplined program of training and practice in order to be successful.

Any attempt to estimate Vengerova's place in the history of piano pedagogy and pianism would require a comparison of her work with that of other teachers, a task which goes beyond the scope of my study. All aspects of her teaching should be covered, not just her method. Certainly any judgment of the latter's qualities would have to consider the following five issues:

(1) The ease with which her method can be learned

(2) Its success in developing a student's technique and musicianship

(3) Its usefulness in performance

(4) The amount of time pianists need to maintain their technique and repertory using her system in comparison to others

(5) The facility with which new material can be learned using it

If I may be allowed to submit a tentative conclusion, I would say that the Vengerova method appears to score very well on the last four points. The first one is more difficult to evaluate. While some learned her system with relatively little trouble, others acquired it only with difficulty, if at all. (But many of the last group may have begun with serious technical problems.) It is, furthermore, one thing to grasp the basic technique and another to apply it with fluency and musical subtlety to difficult works. The application takes longer regardless of how one learns to play the piano. An assessment of this issue has also been clouded by the negative effect Vengerova's personality had on many pupils. Beyond doubt, a teacher with sensitivity, tact, and flexibility can make the adjustment to the Vengerova system easier.

How much is her method being used today? Do her pupils still play and teach that way, or do they modify or discard her system? Joseph Rezits began to explore these questions in his recent article in the *Piano Quarterly,* "Can a 2nd Generation Method Be Successful? The Teaching of Isabelle Vengerova."[24] The replies submitted by thirty-two former Vengerova pupils to his questionnaire suggest that all three positions can be found.

Inevitably after a major figure dies, particularly in a field like piano pedagogy, there is bound to be some lessening of that individual's influence. Changes creep into the performance and teaching of disciples. This in itself is not necessarily bad, for nothing is more deadly than a rigid conservatism without growth, a conservatism which keeps what existed in the past for its own sake without regard for its merit.

But, as historians have long known, the meritorious is often forgotten because there is insufficient record of it. In regard to Vengerova's way of playing the piano, perpetuation by oral tradition alone has been insufficient to insure that her ideas receive their proper attention in the world of pianism. I hope that this book will rectify that situation. It should also help those studying the development of piano playing and teaching by providing information about an important pedagogue.

[24]No. 106 (Summer 1979), pp. 16-23.

This obituary appeared in the *New York Herald Tribune* on Sunday, March 4, 1956 in Section 4, page 5. It is reprinted with permission.

Piano Teacher, Genius
Isabelle Vengerova Died
And Music Lost a 'Great'

Genius is a mystery. It is today, has been in the past, will be in the future. Discussing it, therefore, is a cause of frustration for writers, since words grow numb in trying to describe what makes greatness great.

Recently, to cite a single instance, a great lady died, and the authors of her obituaries were able to do no more than coldly list her achievements. Her name was Madame Isabelle Vengerova; her trade, piano teacher. At once that tells the whole story and also conceals a basic and pertinent fact–she was a genius, the foremost piano pedagogue of her time. For Madame Vengerova had it within her power to take an untrained talent and carve it into something vital and profound. She was, in short, inspired—and her inspiration she drummed into her pupils.

"Better Turn to Stone"

Describing Madame Vengerova, as a result, is something of a chore, for her true gifts were known only to persons whose contacts with her were immediate and direct. Mine were neither. I first met her many years ago when I had chosen criticism over tootling on an oboe. When she heard of my decision, she bristled and scowled. "A critic," she snorted. "Better he should turn to stone."

Thus I am not able to speak personally of Madame Vengerova, as she subsequently regarded me a potential menace. But out of respect for one of the leading figures in her field, I have asked a handful of her pupils to answer briefly one question–

what made the Russian-born Isabelle Vengerova, a professor of piano at Philadelphia's Curtis Institute who died Feb. 7 at seventy-eight, so monumental a teacher?

From composer Samuel Barber came this reply:

"Studying piano with Madame Vengerova was not simply to study with a great teacher. One entered into a life-long love affair with the piano, with all the exigencies, delights and tortures involved in such a relationship.

"I began to study with her at fourteen and I often think that she taught me— through the piano—more about singing than my singing teacher, or more about the construction of a phrase or a movement than my composition teacher... .

"Later in my studies, as I grew older, I could appreciate her loyal friendship, her warm wit and irony. But the first lessons were not easy. With what affection and sadness I remember them: 'Sit still! That piano stool is not a garden swing.' And 'Are you lazy or conceited or just stupid?' Do teachers talk that way today? Sometimes I wish they would."

From conductor - composer - pianist Leonard Bernstein there emerged another view:

"Madame Vengerova never made any separation between technique and expressivity. When she taught piano technique she taught it as a part of the interpretive quality of music—she made your technique grow out of the musical values of each individual piece. You know, it's

(Continued on next page)

much harder to teach that way.

A Tyrant

"It's easy to give some one strong fingers through constant practice of scales, and then to make the matter of interpretation a whole different issue. Some teachers simply build a basic technique which can later be applied to all music. But not Madame. With her the way you played had to come out of the music you played. ...And she was a regular tyrant about it."

Thomas Scherman, conductor of the Little Orchestra Society, had this to say:

"She was a tremendous disciplinarian, so much so that a great many potential students couldn't take the rules she insisted on. . . . She was a sensitive psychologist and treated each student as a distinct case. I think she could have stopped teaching at any time and become a psychologist and made a fortune.

"For one thing, she took each pupil individually—and though she had a distinct teaching method it could be applied to each student differently. She also acted as an artistic conscience for every pupil until each could develop a conscience of his own."

Among the pupils who studied piano with Madame Vengerova and did not turn to allied musical fields are Gary Graffman, Jacob Lateiner, Abba Bogin, Sylvia Zaremba, Lilian Kallir and dozens of other young virtuosi. Polling them all would be a life-time job. Here, however, are the comments contributed by a few of Madame Vengerova's most successful charges.

Her Traditions

Said Mr. Graffman: "She was a combination of all sorts of things. For instance, she combined the romantic tradition of the nineteenth century of which she was a product through her own study with Leschetizky and the twentieth century tradition that demands respect for a composer's wishes. . . . And don't think she only lectured to her students. She was a great pianist herself and to make her ideas clear she would frequently sit down and demonstrate exactly what she meant.

"But most important of all, she taught students how to practice, how to go home and *learn* through practice. She made you understand how it was possible to get the effects you wanted by yourself. . . ."

From Miss Zaremba:

"Madame Vengerova inspired in every student confidence in her sincerity and authoritative criticism. . . . In her eyes there was no final perfection and studying with her was therefore an unending search for the indefinable—a search that resulted in a constant musical growth on the part of all her students."

And Miss Kallir:

"She had a great personality and it was dedicated to teaching; with that went huge insight and perception and no end of vitality. And she was a fantastic craftsman who knew everything there was to know about the piano and the technique of playing it."

Finally from Mr. Bogin:

"I never saw any one who could concentrate the way Madame did. The student was seldom aware that he had released the pedal one thirty-second note sooner or later than the hand, but somehow Madame always heard it. Then she would stop the student and remark, 'Is it possible that I am forty years older than you and have better hearing?' After a day of teaching seven or eight hours, she still had this concentration for the full sixty minutes of an hour lesson."

These, then, are thumbnail descriptions of the essence of genius as told by those on whom this genius has worked its spell. In consequence, it is a fiction to think that Isabelle Vengerova is dead. She lives in every note her pupils play.

APPENDIX B
A LIST OF WORKS STUDIED WITH VENGEROVA

I am including this material to give some idea of the types of pieces she chose to develop a student's technique and musicianship. With such a purpose in mind, it would be most helpful for me to list compositions in the order in which they were studied. This I have done to the best of my ability.

Unfortunately, however, I did not record in my music when each piece was begun. Often I can remember because of my various associations with the work. In other cases there are references in my notebooks, clearly marked by date, which have assisted me in placing a piece chronologically. But since this is not true for all works, it appears best to group them according to some major divisions in my personal and musical life, e.g., where I was living at the time, since I can associate each work clearly with the appropriate grouping. More specific detail is given in parentheses whenever possible. An exact date means that I had a lesson on the work at that time. An asterisk indicates that the work was not selected by Vengerova.

I. Fall 1944—Jan. 1946

First 3 pieces:	Bach: Prelude and Fugue in C Minor from Bk. I, W.T.C.
	Beethoven: Sonata in E^b Major, Op. 7
	Chopin: Etude in A^b Major, Op. 25, No. 1
Bach:	Preludes and Fugues in D Major and D Minor from Bk. I., W.T.C.
Beethoven:	Rondo in G Major, Op. 51, No. 2
Chopin:	Impromptu in A^b Major, Op. 29
	Nocturne in F Minor, Op. 55, No. 1
Clementi:	Etudes from the *Gradus ad Parnassum*
Czerny:	Etudes from Op. 740
Mendelssohn:	Etude in B^b Minor, Op. 104, No. 1
	Rondo Cappriccioso, Op. 14 (Fall 1945)
Moszkowski:	Etudes from Op. 72
Mozart:	Fantasy in C Minor, K. 475 (Fall 1945)
Prokofiev:	March, Op. 12, No. 1
	Vision Fugitive, Op. 22, No. 16
Schumann:	Faschingsschwank aus Wien, Op. 26
	Novellette in F Major, Op. 21, No. 1

I did not study with Vengerova from February 1946 through August 1947.

II. 1947-48

Bach:	Fantasy in C Minor
	*English Suite in G Minor
*Beethoven:	Sonata in E Minor, Op. 90
Chopin:	Fantasie-Impromptu, Op. 66
Clementi:	Etudes from the *Gradus ad Parnassum*
Czerny:	Etudes from Op. 740
Debussy:	Reflets dans l'eau
Kabalevsky:	Sonatina in C Major, Op. 13, No. 1
Mendelssohn:	Etude in F Major, Op. 104, No. 2
Moszkowski:	Etudes from Op. 72
Mozart:	Sonata in C Minor, K. 457
*Poulenc:	Suite in C Major
*Schubert:	Sonata in A Major, Op. 120

III. 1948-51

Bach:	Preludes and Fugues in *E^b Minor, F# Minor, G Minor (Fall 1948), G# Minor, from Bk. I, W.T.C.
Beethoven:	Concerto No. 1 in C Major, Op. 15
Brahms:	Ballade in D Minor, Op. 10, No. 1
	*Cappriccio in G Minor, Op. 116, No. 3
	*Intermezzo in E Major, Op. 116, No. 4
	Intermezzo in E^b Major, Op. 117, No. 1
	Rhapsody in G Minor, Op. 79, No. 2 (23 Dec 49)
Chopin:	*Ballade in A^b Major, Op. 47 (Fall 1950)
	Etudes in C# Minor, Op. 10, No. 4 (7 Sept 49); *F Major, Op. 10, No. 8 (20 Dec 48); C Minor, Op. 10, No. 12 (Fall 1948); F Minor, Op. 25, No. 2
Debussy:	Jardins sous la pluie (23 Dec 49)
Liszt:	Un Sospiro (5 Mar 50)
	Waldesrauschen (Fall 1950)
Medtner:	Fairy Tale, Op. 34, No. 2
Mendelssohn:	Etude in A Minor, Op. 104, No. 3 (Fall 1948)
	Fantasy in F# Minor, Op. 28
	Scherzo a Cappriccio in F# Minor (9 Jan 49)
Moszkowski:	En automne, Op. 36, No. 4

Rachmaninoff:	Elegie, Op. 3, No. 1 (5 Mar 50)
	Prelude in E^b Major, Op. 23, No. 6 (24 June 50)
Schumann:	Novellette in E Major, Op. 21, No. 7 (20 Dec 48)
	Sonata in G Minor, Op. 22 (Fall 1949)
Weber:	Perpetual Motion (from the Sonata Op. 24)

IV. 1951-53

Bach:	Preludes and Fugues in *C# Minor and *C# Major, from Bk. I, W.T.C.
Beethoven:	Sonata in D Minor, Op. 31, No. 2 (30 Nov 52)
Brahms:	Intermezzo in B^b Minor, Op. 117, No. 2
Chopin:	Etudes in G^b Major, Op. 10, No. 5 and C Minor, Op. 25, No. 12
	Mazurkas in F# Minor, Op. 6, No. 1; B^b Major, Op. 17, No. 1; *C# Minor, Op. 41, No. 1
	Scherzo in C# Minor, Op. 39
Debussy:	La soirée dans Grenade
*Mozart:	Sonata in A Minor, K. 310
Prokofiev:	Prelude in C Major, Op. 12, No. 7
	Sonata No. 3 in A Minor, Op. 28 (Spring 1953)
*Rubinstein:	Staccato Etude in C Major, Op. 23, No. 2
*Schubert:	Impromptu in B^b Major, Op. 142, No. 3 (9 Jan 53)
*Schumann:	Papillons, Op. 2

I entered the army in the summer of 1953 and did not resume lessons with Vengerova until about March 1954.

V. 1954-56

(Vengerova died on February 7, 1956. I had my last lesson with her on January 1, 1956.)

*Bach-Busoni:	Two Chorale Preludes: Nun komm' der Heiden Heiland, and Nun freut euch, Lieben Christen
*Beethoven:	Sonata in E Major, Op. 109 (Fall 1955)
Chopin:	Etudes in D^b Major, Op. 25, No. 8 (Fall 1955) and G^b Major, Op. 25, No. 9
Kabalevsky:	Sonata No. 3 in F Major, Op. 46

*Kennan, Kent:	Three Preludes
Moszkowski:	Etude in G^b Major, Op. 24, No. 1
Paganini-Liszt:	Etude No. 6 (1 Jan 56)
*Schumann:	Concerto in A Minor, Op. 54

APPENDIX C
VITALY NEUMANN ON VENGEROVA'S TEACHING IN RUSSIA

The following essay about Vengerova's teaching in Russia was written by the late Vitaly Neumann, a Soviet pianist and music scholar, who found his source material in the archives of the Leningrad Conservatory where Vengerova's personal correspondence is kept. Her nephew, Nicolas Slonimsky, translated and sent it to me in the form given here. He said that the article is almost complete though he omitted some transitions between paragraphs. Those sentences which are not in quotation marks are by him. Although excerpts have appeared in at least two places,[25] this is, to the best of my knowledge, the most complete version to be printed so far.

In one of her letters of 1905, Vengerova gives a vivid report about piano teaching at the Smolnyi Institute, a school for daughters of the Russian nobility in Leningrad: "The girls are very nice, but they haven't any talent. My salary is satisfactory but there is an enormous amount of work to do. I get up at seven o'clock in the morning; it takes an hour to get to the Smolnyi. Classes begin at nine, and I finish at about half past one. Then I give several private lessons at home and practice myself about three hours. I must also go out to parties and receive guests, so that my life is rather full."

In 1906 Vengerova was engaged as an instructor at the St. Petersburg Conservatory. She wrote to her mother at the time: "Music takes up eleven hours of my day, and I sometimes feel very tired. I have 45 students, of whom 20 are at the Conservatory, and 25 are private."

"The pedagogical talent of Isabelle Vengerova was developed in all its brilliance during her professorship at the St. Petersburg Conservatory," Vitaly Neumann writes. "Her influence on her students was profound. She creatively elaborated the pedagogical principles of her own teachers Leschetizky and Anna Essipova, but introduced also her individual characteristics. The position of the hands, which Vengerova regarded as most important in piano technique, was characterized by the following:

[25]Reginald Gerig, *Famous Pianist and Their Technique* (Washington: Robert B. Luce, Inc., 1974), pp. 312-13; and Joseph Rezits, "Can a 2nd Generation Method Be Successful? The Teaching of Isabelle Vengerova," *The Piano Quarterly,* No. 106 (Summer 1979), pp. 18-19.

"(1) The elbows to be kept away from the torso, (2) The wrists to be held with complete freedom, (3) The fingers to maintain a curved position, with strength and precision. Vengerova paid particular attention to the necessity of quick removal of a finger from the key immediately after it is struck, and instantly shifting it to the position above the next key to be played. Vengerova devoted much effort to the digital technique, and also gave instruction for the coordination of the movements of the fingers with the motions of the forearm, which she regarded as imperative in order to attain a variety and richness of instrumental sonority."

"Vengerova made high professional demands on her students. Every new piece had to be played from memory at the very first lesson. 'Do not try to interpret the music with a definite expression on the beginning,' she used to tell her pupils. Nuances, articulation, phrasing and other particulars, she maintained, should derive from a deep emotional feeling and understanding of the style, and should not be mechanically attached to the notes, following a teacher's instruction or the editor's indications in the music."

"Work over details of performance was conducted with great care in Vengerova's class. The student was expected to grasp the harmonic scheme and formal structure of the music, and to bring out climaxes. Each melodic inflection was carefully analyzed, with minute attention paid to the ear's control over the contrapuntal and harmonic parts. In her classes Vengerova invariably played the pieces under study to demonstrate the proper interpretation of the music. Her knowledge of piano literature was extraordinary, and she could play from memory the entire pedagogical repertory. By her own performance for her students she strove to stimulate their imagination, to awaken a personal interest in the music. Fifty years after Vengerova left Russia, one of her conservatory pupils remembered Vengerova's playing of Schumann's Novellette No. 8, imaginatively evoking the romantic poetry of Schumann's visions."

"Vengerova demanded from her students constant improvement in their general and musical culture. She tried to impart to her students her own qualities of independence, intellectual discipline and liberality of personal opinion. 'When you play a Beethoven Sonata, you must also form an idea of all other Beethoven Sonatas,' Vengerova used to say. 'While playing a work of a certain composer you must become familiar with the historical era of his time, his biography, his ideas and musicians who influenced his creative imagination. You must also study scholarly and literary works devoted to this composer.' "

108

"In her class, students had weekly lessons, but other students were expected to be present at her lessons. This enabled the entire class to acquire a wide knowledge of piano literature and to have an opportunity to absorb her pedagogical methods. By playing in front of others, students were prepared for future public appearances. In her choice of works, Vengerova concentrated on the classical and romantic periods. Haydn, Mozart, Beethoven, Chopin, Schumann, Tschaikovsky, Brahms and Liszt were constantly studied, but she also gave to her students works by contemporary Russians—Glazunov, Rachmaninoff, Medtner and early Scriabin. But she determinedly excluded all second-rate composers and salon-type popular music for the piano."

Bibliography

Books and Articles

A. A. C. Review of Mme. Essipoff's New York debut on 14 November 1876. *Dwight's Journal of Music* 36 (25 November, 1876):343.

Brée, Malwine. *The Groundwork of the Leschetizky Method, Issued with His Approval by His Assistant Malwine Brée.* Translated by Th. Baker. New York: G. Schirmer, 1902.

Dyer, Richard. "For di Bonaventura, virtuosity not enough." *Boston Sunday Globe,* 8 October 1972.
    An interview containing two paragraphs about Anthony di Bonaventura's study with Vengerova.

Encyclopaedia Judaica. S.v. "Wengeroff, Pauline," by Yehuda Slutzky, and "Wengeroff (Vengerov), Semyon Afanasyevich," by Maurice Friedberg.

Flissler, Eileen. "The Venerable Vengerova: Magician of Pianoforte." *Music Journal* 23 (March 1965): 32.

Furney, Mabel McDonough. "Detroit Symphony Gains New Success." *Musical America* 41 (21 February 1925): 9.

Gát, József. *The Technique of Piano Playing,* 2nd ed. London: Collet's Holdings Ltd., 1965.

Gerig, Reginald. *Famous Pianists and Their Technique.* Washington: Robert B. Luce, Inc., 1974.

Graffman, Gary. *I Really Should Be Practicing.* Garden City, NY: Doubleday and Co., 1981.
    An autobiography which devotes considerable space to Graffman's lessons with Vengerova.

Helland, Dave, and Doerschuk, Bob. "Gary Graffman: Classical Eclecticist." *Contemporary Keyboard* 4 (December 1978): 18.
    An interview containing several paragraphs about Graffman's study with Vengerova.

Neal, Harry Lee. "The Unforgettable Vengerova." *The Piano Teacher* 4 (September-October 1961): 2-4.

_____. *Wave as You Pass.* Philadelphia: J. B. Lippincott Co., 1958. Chapter on Isabelle Vengerova.

Ortmann, Otto. *The Physical Basis of Piano Touch and Tone.* London: Kegan, Paul, Trench, Trubner, and Co., Ltd., 1925.

Overtones. Vols. 1-10 (1929-1939).
A publication of the Curtis Institute of Music which contains frequent references to Vengerova.

Petri, Egon. "Problems of Piano Playing and Teaching," in *Be Your Own Music Critic,* ed. Robert E. Simon, Jr. Garden City, NY: Doubleday, Doran, and Co., Inc., 1941.

Rezits, Joseph. "Can a 2nd Generation Method Be Successful? The Teaching of Isabelle Vengerova." *The Piano Quarterly,* no. 106 (Summer 1979), pp. 16-23.

_____. "Lessons with Vengerova." *The Piano Teacher* 8 (November-December 1965): 2-5.

Schnabel, Artur. *My Life and Music.* New York: St. Martin's Press, 1963.

Slonimsky, Nicolas. " 'Musique': Reminiscences of a vanished world." *The Piano Teacher* 6 (September-October 1963): 2-4.

_____. *Baker's Biographical Dictionary of Musicians,* 6th ed. S.v. "Vengerova, Isabelle."

Vengerova, Isabelle. "The Piano as It Seems to Me." *Overtones* 1 (February 1930): 114-16.

Webster's Third New International Dictionary of the English Language Unabridged, S.v. "Method."

Volumes with Exercises

Chopin, Frederic. *Twelve Studies,* Op. 10, ed. Alfred Cortot. Paris: Editions Salabert, 1915.

_____. *Twelve Studies,* Op. 25, ed. Alfred Cortot. Paris: Editions Salabert, 1917.

Döring, Carl Heinrich. *Exercises and Studies on the Pianoforte for the Preparation and Development of Staccato Octave Playing.* New York: G. Schirmer, 1902.

Joseffy, Rafael. *Daily Studies on the Piano.* New York: E. Schuberth and Co., 1880.

Moszkowski, Moritz. *School of Scales and Double Notes for the Piano,* Bks. II and III. London: Enoch & Co., 1901.

Pischna, J. *Technical Studies for the Piano.* New York: G. Schirmer, 1904.

Tausig, Carl. *Daily Studies for the Piano,* ed. H. Ehrlich. New York: G. Schirmer, n.d.

INDEX

The Preface, Appendix B, and the Bibliography were not indexed. A page number in italics indicates a musical example.

About the Author

Robert D. Schick was born in 1929 in New York City where he attended the High School of Music and Art. He holds a bachelor's degree from Swarthmore College, a master's with a major in music composition from Columbia University, and a Doctor of Musical Arts with a major in piano performance and pedagogy from the Eastman School of Music.

His studies with Mme. Vengerova began in 1944 and continued until her death in 1956, except for two intervals totalling about two years when he was away.

Performing as a solo pianist, accompanist, and chamber musician is important to him. Aesthetics, music criticism, and ethnomusicology are among his other interests. He has served as a part-time critic and is now writing a book about music criticism.

Since 1959 he has been a college teacher, first at Chatham College and, since 1961, at West Chester State College where he is Professor of Piano. With his wife and two sons he resides in West Chester, Pennsylvania.